Screwed Up, Slimmed Down

JENNA WIMSHURST

Copyright © 2023 Jenna Wimshurst

All rights reserved.

ISBN: 9798865055211

I'd like to dedicate this book to my therapist, our
sessions have been priceless.

(Only in theory of course, in reality they're £50 a pop.
But still, I couldn't have gotten through this hellish year
without you.)

CONTENTS

Chapter		Page
	Nice to Meet You. Probably…	1
1	I've Got Enough on My Plate, Apparently	6
2	Walt Disney Can Go and Fuck Himself	12
3	Watch Out for the Eternal Thrush	21
4	Introducing Jenna's Form of Keto	27
5	Hypnotherapy by the Sex Pool	34
6	We Are the Fruitcakes of Our Mother's Loin	39
7	EVERYTHING IS OK, DON'T PANIC!	46
8	I Am a Pretty Little Flower	50
9	Hove, Actually…	53
10	Taking Life One Antidepressant at a Time	57
11	Has My Loneliness Peaked Yet?	62
12	I'm Duller Than a Clipboard	69
13	The Fat Just Melts Off	75
14	My Fanny Has Died	80
15	My Guinea Pig Is in the Bloody Way	82
16	There'll Be No Sex in This Hot Tub	85

SCREWED UP, SLIMMED DOWN

17	Wow, This Sucks…	89
18	My Cup of Self-Care Is Bloody Empty…	92
19	Spain Will Delay My Pain	98
20	Death Would've Been Easier	103
21	Less Fat, More Sad	105
22	Feelings Suck…	109
23	Don't Ask the Therapist About Her Vagina	111
24	I'm No Longer Obese	115
25	How to Work 9–5 and Not Shoot Yourself in the Face	118
26	Fill Up My Pockets and Empty Out My Soul	123
27	Hannah Broke My Heart	126
28	No Strings Attached	133
29	I Am Not the Lesbian Nadal	136
30	Self-Worth With Next-Day Delivery	139
31	I Am Now a Medium	144
32	Am I a Shit Shag?	148
33	My Inner Child Needs to Shut It	151
34	An English Muffin in Denver	155
35	Another Human Being Likes Me	163

SCREWED UP, SLIMMED DOWN

36	Goodbye to the Old Jenna	172
37	The New Jenna Has Arrived	176
38	Lucky Number Four	180
39	I Quit My Job, Shit…	182
40	Any Five Foot Ten Paramedics in the House?	187
41	The Best Day of the Year	190
42	Thirty-Eight Inches of Pure Sex Appeal	196
43	The First Birthday on My Own	198
44	It's Called Fashion, Dickhead	203
45	I Can Fill Up My Own Cup, Thank You	206
46	Twelve Stone and Thirteen Pounds of Fabulousness	212
47	Goodbye My Fluffy Little Nubbin	213
48	A Big lezzy Wedding	217
49	Wreath It and Weep	223
50	Thank Fuck That's Over	230
51	Three Desserts and a Beard	235
	Acknowledgements	241
	About the Author	243

NICE TO MEET YOU. PROBABLY…

'Why write a book about being a fat, depressed lesbian who wants to change her life?' I hear you cry. Well, if you could please keep the crying to a minimum while you read this book, that would be great. Unless of course you're crying with laughter, in which case, go ahead and bawl your bloody eyes out.

Hi, I'm Jenna and I'm a lesbian and, yes, that is the most interesting thing about me. I'm also a five foot nine Mediterranean-looking English woman who suffers from both depression and anxiety, which I used to think made me quite unique, but since mental health has become less of a taboo, it seems that everyone has some sort of mental fuggery going on. So, really, I'm not special at all…

That makes me sad. I was already sad – but now I'm sadder… Am I sadder than everyone else? It certainly feels like it. Yay, there you go – I'm special again!

Anyhoo… my hobbies include indicating, fantasising about Rafael Nadal's left bicep (which is a bit odd for a lesbian – I mean, I shouldn't really be thinking about any of Nadal's body parts) and telling my guinea pigs to stop pooing in their food bowl.

But, back to my depression… I've had it since my early teens (I've been a lesbian since then as well, but it took me years to realise because I was too busy giving buzz cuts to Barbies), so let's just say that I'm no stranger to feeling like the sack of mouldy, shit potatoes that my dad would say are still OK to eat.

However, I've finally had enough. I have coasted my way to 32 without putting any thought or effort into making my short time on this rock a happy or fulfilling one. My life is small, my panic attacks are huge… and I feel like nothing good is ever going to happen again. I'm just waiting for my real life to begin, but not in a Hindu reincarnation sort of way, more a 'I need to stop crying myself silly every night and actually start doing something with my life' sort of way.

Let me explain…

For the last five years, I've worked from home doing a marketing job which fills me with dread. My relationship with my family is more strained than the last teabag shared between five thirsty builders, and things between my partner and I have been slowly deteriorating since our wedding was cancelled due to the 'C' word. (That's Covid, not c*nt. Oh God, I've gone and written c*nt at the beginning of the book, I do apologise.)

To say that I don't have many friends would be an understatement. I can count the number of my friends on one hand. In fact, I could cut off all my fingers and still be able to count them on one hand. Except that would be worse because then I'd be both friendless *and* fingerless – thankfully I'm just friendless, otherwise this book would take even longer to write.

Just in case you were sitting there trying to imagine what I look like naked, let me paint you a picture – I'm fat. Like really quite fat – I eat my feelings, you see, and there's a lot of feelings to eat.

In fact, sometimes I have so many feelings that I want to walk into the sea. Which is a weird thing to say really, because there comes a point when you're in the sea… walking… and it gets so deep that you have to start swimming. But saying that you want to swim in the sea doesn't sound like you're suicidal, it sounds like you're into wild swimming. Which I guess is the same thing.

But everything is about to change, because the other day, while I was sitting on the toilet scrolling through Instagram during another boring New Year's Eve at home, I came across a 10-second clip of actress Rebel Wilson saying that she'd lost five stone after deciding that 2020 was going to be her year of health.

Suddenly, I was filled with inspiration… (I was also filled with poo because all of those Christmas binges had really backed me up). But it was during that moment that I had a constipated epiphany. 'I am no longer going to just exist in this sad, miserable life, I'm actually going to start living. This next year is going to be *my year*,' I declared to myself before getting up to wipe.

The new sexy, amazing Jenna starts today. I just need to lose a serious amount of weight, stop feeling like a bag of pessimistic poop and actually leave my flat. Sounds easy, right? Except for the fact that I've got all the self-control of an unattended garden hose and all the motivation of a dead squirrel.

My goal for my physical health is to lose between three and four stone and, like Adele, I hope to transform into someone so skinny that people will be like 'OMG! I hope you didn't lose your sense of humour.' But don't worry, because – apparently – you can't lose something you never had…

My goal for my mental health is to be able to feel something other than total despair. My life for the past five years has been extremely isolated – that's right, I was isolating before it was a government mandate. But I'm fed up of doing nothing and feeling empty inside.

I dream of a time when I have a lovely group of friends that I go out with, where I'm my authentic self who happens to be effortlessly funny and not a shy little beaver who people-pleases. I'd like to spend my weekends exploring places and having all the mad sex with my partner, Cat, rather than just sitting on the sofa waiting for the kindness of death to save me from the pain of life.

So, dear reader, are you still here? Oh, how lovely! Why don't you join me on my transformation journey from fat, depressed lesbian, to, hopefully, just a lesbian?

Oh God, I almost forgot! We won't be alone on this ride…

Inside of me there are two other people (not like that, you pervert). There's Earl, the depressed megalomaniac – he's a real delight. Allow me to give you an example. Just the other day I was sitting on the sofa, eating my sixth bag of large chocolate buttons, or 'dinner' if you want to call it that, when suddenly a twinge made its way across my back.

Earl: That's spinal cancer.
Me: Or it's just a weird twinge.
Earl: 12th stage, I reckon.
Me: …
Earl: You've probably only got five weeks left to live.
Me: …
Earl: Six at a push.
Me: If it happens again, I'll go to the doctor – I'm sure it'll be fine.
Earl: One day the sun will engulf the earth and there'll be no trace of anyone's existence, so really, how is anything fine?

The other person inside me is the jubilant, wild Wanda. She can go between being the voice of reason to being like an excited little puppy who's swallowed 12 LSD tablets and just wants to experience everything, everywhere, at all once.

SCREWED UP, SLIMMED DOWN

Allow me to give you an example... Just the other day I was sitting on the sofa, eating my sixth bag of large chocolate buttons, or 'dinner' if you want to call it that, when suddenly a twinge made its way across my back.

Wanda: OMG! You should totally go and try base jumping!
Me: What the hell is base jumping?
Wanda: It's where you jump off buildings.
Me: But what about the back twinge that I just had?
Wanda: That's not base jumping.
Me: No, but shouldn't I worry about it?
Wanda: Maybe you should try parkour first, and then upgrade to base jumping.
Me: Oh God, I think the twinge is back again. What if it's cancer?
Wanda: Then you should skip parkour and go straight to base jumping! Yeah – base jumping! Woo hoo!

And then there's me. I'm the captain of this weird human-shaped ship and I don't really have much say in how it's run. I just listen to whoever is loudest.

So, with these two idiots in tow, I'm ready to restart my life and do things again, properly this time, less fannying about doing nothing and more fannying about doing something.

This book that you are just about to read (unless you're horrendously offended by the C word I mentioned earlier) is about how I plan to start again, as the new me. If I was an American or an Instagram influencer (which you'll be shocked to read that I'm not) then I would say that this is my journey to living my #BestLife, or any life worth living really...

CHAPTER 1

I'VE GOT ENOUGH ON MY PLATE, APPARENTLY

January

For the first 32 years of my life my diet has been indistinguishable from the food served at your average five-year-old's birthday party, and if I carry on living like this then I'm going to die of all the cancers by the time I hit 35.

I'm two stone overweight. And if I put *both* feet on the scales then I'm actually *four stone* overweight (after a massive dump of course – oh, how uncouth, I'm so sorry). Being fat makes me tired, miserable and unhappy. I've always been a bit chubby – in fact, my mother was induced two weeks early because I was getting so big in the womb. It really was a sign of things to come.

Life would be so much easier if I could just learn to love my big round stomach – just like those body-positive influencers do. But, I'm afraid I can't bring myself to be positive about my flabby belly, my thunderous thighs and my bingo wings that cause me to take off every time I wave at someone.

SCREWED UP, SLIMMED DOWN

I remember being nine years old and sitting in the school dining hall talking to my equally chubby best friend about how unhappy I was that I was the biggest girl in my class.

'Don't worry, it's just puppy fat, it'll go when we're adults,' she assured me.

'How do you know that?' I asked.

'Fat Shelley told me.'

Well, mine and (it turns out after some Facebook stalking) Fat Shelley's puppy fat *never* went.

Four years later, I was sitting on my sofa a few days before my 13th birthday when my mum handed me a present.

'You can open this one early,' she said, which even super-emo Jenna was over the moon about. I shook it. It rattled – definitely not chocolate then. I ripped open the paper and staring back at me was my first mobile phone. This was in the very early days of mobile phones, it didn't even have a Quadcore Super-Dragon processor for all my gaming and multitasking needs. *Can... you... believe?*

'Thanks, Mum,' I grinned happily.

'You're welcome,' she said. 'I was going to say I'll give it to you if you lost weight and got down to 11 stone, but I decided not to.' (I was 11 and a half stone at the time.)

'Oh, OK. Thank you,' I said, looking down at my feet, ashamed. 'I promise I'll lose weight,' I whimpered, the smile very much gone from my face.

Teenage Jenna was so unhappy in her own skin that she felt that her mum was probably right in giving her that challenge at such a young age. It's only 19 years later that I realise how upsetting that situation was.

If I had a psychology degree (which you'll be shocked to learn that I don't), I would say that this could have, quite possibly, contributed to me feeling ugly and horrendously self-conscious about my body. If my mum is reading this, then a) I'm super happy (and surprised) that you've made it this far into the book and, b) you need to

SCREWED UP, SLIMMED DOWN

make it up to me by buying me the latest iPhone for the next 50 years.

My friend telling me that all I had was puppy fat was the first time I realised that I was a properly fat child (though looking back now I would *die* to be that size again, which is funny because if I *did* die then I would eventually get back down to that size #DeathGoals). It was when I was 24 years old, sitting in my dad's living room watching some crap Saturday night TV, that I realised that I was a properly fat adult.

'I'm going to buy the new blue Rafael Nadal jacket from Nike,' I told my dad as I chomped down on a slice of pizza.

'What! Jeeez, how much is that?' he asked, forever concerned with how much things are.

'It's £65.'

'How much?!' he shrieked, in the way only a bloke from Peckham can shriek (think Del Boy, but more common).

'I've got the money.'

'Yeah, but there's no point in getting an expensive jacket, because it's not going to look nice on you.' I put the slice of pizza back into the box and closed it, the feeling of ugliness sinking deep within me.

He might've been right, but, if I had a psychology degree (which you'll be shocked to learn that I *still* don't), I would say that this is why since that day I've only worn cheap clothes that are black and *at least* two sizes too big for me. If my dad is reading this, then a) I'm super happy (and surprised) that you've made it this far into the book, and b) you need to make it up to me by buying me Rafael Nadal's latest tennis outfit for the next 50 years.

It was during my time working at a pizza restaurant after university that I put on most of my adult blubber. The job only paid £5.50 an hour, but that was OK because I gained an extra four pounds every shift.

I mainly eat when I'm depressed. I like the way the

food tastes, how it makes me feel – and I love it when I haven't eaten for at *least* half an hour because that means that it will soon be time to eat again.

I've indulged in many a food binge in my life. There have been multiple times that I've innocently popped to the shop for a small wee bar of chocolate and left with six cookies, three Twixs and two tubs of ice cream. I would then sit on my bed and scoff the lot. You can imagine how awful I felt mentally afterwards… I wouldn't wish that feeling on anyone. Well, apart from the friend who said I'd lose my puppy fat when I became an adult – lying bitch.

Diet is *so* important when it comes to mental health that literally 10s of people have written books about it. Apparently, there's a link between our diet, exercise and our mood. I know! I'm as shocked as you are.

So, if I'm going to change my mental and physical health, then I need to start by improving my diet and doing more exercise.

> **Earl:** Jesus, no one needs to see your fat arse jiggling about.
> **Me:** Oh, thank you so much for the support.
> **Earl:** Anytime. Talking of support, may I suggest you get an industrial-strength sports bra?
> **Me:** No, you may not.
> **Wanda:** Let's sign up for an ultramarathon!
> **Me and Earl:** Shut up, Wanda.

The only thing that concerns me about losing weight (apart from the fact that it's super hard and boring) is that it might give those arseholes satisfaction. You know the arseholes I'm talking about – the ones where according to them nothing is worse than being fat and they wouldn't hire you for a job over someone who's thin because thinness shows self-control and good character. Which is funny because some of the biggest pricks I know are thin, and I wouldn't hire them to shit in a toilet let alone anything else.

Well, my plan is to:

Eat a healthy and well-balanced diet: I'm not sure what this is yet, but I imagine it involves eating so much whole grain that I'll start swaying in the wind.

Exercise more: I know, I didn't think that was possible either. I've been to the gym at least five times in my life, but apparently exercise isn't like sex, in the sense that if you've done it once you don't really need to do it again for another year.

Cut down on the delicious food: Because, although life is short, apparently eating sweet and sour prawn balls with chips from the Chinese takeaway every other night makes it even shorter (they don't tell you that on the menu, do they?).

Cut down on other people's bullshit: And by other people's, I mean my own. I'm going to avoid being bored, angry, frustrated and sad, because those emotions make me want to scoff myself into a diabetic coma. I also need to avoid being happy, joyful, excited and indifferent, because those emotions *also* make me want to scoff myself into a diabetic coma.

> **Earl:** You're going to fail miserably at this transformation journey.
> **Me:** Why is that?
> **Earl:** Because you always fail, you get bored and realise that there's no point in achieving anything because achievement is, at best, futile.
> **Me:** I will do this.
> **Earl:** You won't.
> **Me:** Will.

Earl: Won't.

Me: Will.

Earl: Won't.

Me: This is childish. I'm going to lose weight and I'm going to become the best version of myself.

Earl: And what about when you have a bad day? Will the new Jenna be able to cope with that? Or will she stuff her chubby little face with cookies?

Me: Well, let's hope not.

Earl: Hope? What is this 'hope' thing you speak of? Is it like prayer? Are you going to pray away your fat?

Me: Whatever works.

The journey to the shitting-hot new me has begun!

CHAPTER 2

WALT DISNEY CAN GO AND FUCK HIMSELF

I'd like to introduce you to Cat, my partner of eight years. She's from Scotland, but please don't hold that against her. She's a very jolly, positive and spunky woman from Dundee, a place where there's a bloke who stands outside the shopping centre chain-smoking and playing the harmonica simultaneously.

Cat also suffers from anxiety, so when we're both going through anxious episodes… well… it's quite the party. It's bad enough when we get dual PMT and end up aggressively grouting our shower to get our rage out, but add a dollop of anxiety, and our flat turns into an absolute pit of terror. I really do fear for our children sometimes. They're guinea pigs, by the way; they're called Rusty and Tiny Tim and they despise us and everything we stand for – motherhood really is *so* rewarding.

Cat and I met online when I was 24, and five years later I made her climb Arthur's Seat (the huge bastard hill in Edinburgh), where I got down on one knee and asked her to put up with me for the rest of her life. She said alright.

SCREWED UP, SLIMMED DOWN

To say we've moulded into the same person would be an understatement. There have been many times when we've both got ready for a night out (in separate rooms), and arrived by the front door ready to leave in *exactly* the same outfit.

We're both extremely uncool, but in the best way. For example, we went to Amsterdam a few years ago and we did all the drug-taking that you're expected to do (just weed, not the scary stuff). We sat in a coffee shop with a spliff and took turns sucking the life out of it.

'I don't feel any different,' I said.

'Me neither…' she replied.

'Let's do another one,' I suggested as I reached into my pocket and took out the extra spliff we'd bought for the next day.

Thirty minutes later…

'I'm tired. Shall we go and have a nap?' Cat said as we floated down the road.

'Good idea. But let's get munchies on the way.'

'Babe, we've just bought munchies,' she said pointing to the bag of chocolate, crisps and sandwiches that I was holding.

'Oh yeah…' I looked at the bag and bent over giggling like it was the funniest thing that had ever happened.

We popped back to the hotel, laid down for a nap and then six hours later we woke up and agreed that we don't do drugs very well and we should probably not do any more drugs. Instead, we spent the rest of the holiday doing all the tourist bollocks and making love.

Cut to two years ago, just months before our March 2020 wedding…

……

Two years ago

'There's a killer disease in China,' the news reporter said. Yeah, but China is miles away so it doesn't affect us. Then the news said, 'The killer disease is now in South Korea.' Yeah, well, South Korea is even *further* away. Or is it technically nearer? Regardless, there's no need to worry about it impacting our upcoming nuptials.

But then the news reported that the killer disease had arrived in France and I thought perhaps it would be best if we closed the borders, shut the Channel Tunnel and all just hid in the bathroom. We don't want it invading the UK; it's us who does the invading, thank you very much. But, alas, the day came when the killer disease was here in Britain.

'The killer disease has invaded the UK, with thousands dying alone and millions having to amputate their own heads just to stay alive,' said the news. It was something like that anyway – I don't know for sure because I turned the news off a week into lockdown after concluding that my anxiety had been right all along.

The news: There's a global pandemic.
Earl: I told you we were all doomed.
Me: I'm sure it'll go away and we'll all go back to normal.
Earl: You hate normal.
Me: I also hate pandemics.
Earl: There'll be more pandemics in the future.
Me: Yeah, but not for at least another 100 years.
Earl: A boy in Mongolia has just died of bubonic plague.
Me: What's the quickest way to kill myself?
Earl: Attagirl.

Just one week before our wedding day the venue called to inform us that although they were cancelling, they would still be keeping our money as per their terms and conditions, which cover them for anything that could ever possibly happen. But stay safe and don't touch your face!

So with no wedding and no money, what were two gorgeous lesbians supposed to do on the special date that they'd already had engraved on their wedding rings? Host an unofficial wedding in their living room and stream it online, of course.

We decided to do this to a) show our love for each other, b) keep our family and friends' spirits up, and c) not have to give back the cordless Dyson we'd received as an early wedding present. Seriously, it was our favourite thing in the flat besides our guinea pigs. We loved it so much that we'd actually come close to using the damn thing.

You better believe that I turned myself into a shit-hot lawyer (via thousands of YouTube videos, lawyer forums and endless *Orange Is the New Black* episodes) and eventually got the money back from the wedding venue.

Our fake wedding day arrived. Picture the scene – tacky fake ivy and fairy lights dotted around our living room, us wearing our non-returnable 'Wifey 2020' jumpers standing in front of an interestingly decorated table featuring: a wedding cake (Wiggles the caterpillar), a bottle of bubbly (£5, lovely stuff) and a marriage certificate (printed off the internet from some random Mormon website).

It looked lovely and we were all set to go live at two in the afternoon. I just needed to make sure that my 70-year-old mother was on the right Facebook page and not watching some life hack guru teaching her how to change the oil in an 18-wheeler.

'Mum, can you see Cat waving in front of the camera?'

'Which camera?'

'On Facebook, Mum, there's a live video. Are you watching it? Cat is waving to see if you're looking at the right thing.'

'Oh'

'…'

'Yes, I can see someone waving.'

'Great! Now don't breathe or touch anything.'

With three minutes to go the anxiety and emotions had set in. But we were keeping composed... well, we were until Cat's parents sent us a picture of them in their wedding outfits with glasses of bubbly ready for the ceremony that they'd somehow managed to get on their TV. It's good to know that not everyone over the age of 60 needs technical support.

Three... two... one... and we were live. Suddenly my anxiety and doubts started to scream.

Earl: What the fuck are you doing? Don't get married!
Me: Why not?
Earl: Because it's a mistake!
Me: But I love Cat and I want to be with her forever.
Earl: Is she the one, though?
Me: What does that even mean?
Earl: Is she the Cinderella to your Prince Charming?
Me: Am I Prince Charming? Why am I Prince Charming? I want to be Cinderella.
Earl: You definitely shouldn't get married, idiot.
Me: But I love her.
Earl: But does your love feel like the all-consuming obsessive Disney-style love?
Me: No, but... that's not real. Is it?
Earl: Do you still get crazy butterflies when she enters the room?
Me: No, but...
Earl: Do you desperately yearn for her every second of every day?
Me: ...
Earl: I think I've made my point.

Would this have happened on the *actual* wedding day? Shit. What was I doing? It was just a fake ceremony on Facebook and I was freaking out inside. Was she the one? Is there a 'one'? Maybe I should be feeling more...

SCREWED UP, SLIMMED DOWN

'Hello everyone!' we beamed, smiling at the camera; the wedding had begun. The ceremony was beautiful, fun and also really quick – seven minutes in total and we had over 150 people watching (which was more than we had invited to the real ceremony because at £57 per head we had to decide whether we really loved Uncle Robert and his three children that much, or whether they could just come to the evening bit and still bring a gift).

Once the ceremony was over we toasted our new unofficial marriage, got drunk and said goodbye to the livestream so that Cat and I could go and consummate the marriage. And by consummate the marriage, I mean we took a two-hour nap and then played with our new VR set on the PlayStation until 2 am. Cat played a shoot-'em-up war game and I played virtual tennis. It was the first time I'd ever played any sort of tennis (real or virtual) and I loved it so much that I would soon be playing the shit out of it every day. Well, it was lockdown, what else was there to do?

Just one month later Cat lost her job. A job she had sacrificed so much of herself and her time into that it almost broke up our relationship and I considered leaving. Although it's hard to leave someone who is never actually there. She would leave at six in the morning and get home at eight at night – did the boss think of that before he decided to drop her like an unwanted child?

During her time at that job (she works in financial crime, I know, right, fancy bitch) I felt *so* lonely. There she was, going off to London every day having a big exciting time with her colleagues, having lunches out and drinks after work, and there I was, stuck working at home on my own, the highlight of my day being when I got to put the bins out. I know it sounds like I was jealous, but I wasn't. I'd rather have my fingernails slowly pulled out with rusty pliers than commute to London and spend every day in an office.

When she'd eventually get home at night, she'd just sit

on the sofa messaging her colleagues on Slack. She was an empty shell of a woman who didn't really have the energy to chat with me. Whereas I was full of beans having not spoken to a soul all day. I understood that she was shattered after a long day, of course, but, you know… it wasn't great for our relationship.

We had two very different lives and it was no one's fault, but those two lives weren't compatible. So, when she lost her job during the pandemic it was a weird feeling. My darling Cat had lost the big exciting job that she loved, but also, I'd got her back. My wonderful, funny, caring partner.

Lockdown was tough for everyone (apart from the CEOs of Zoom, Amazon and PornHub) but it was during 2020 that our relationship really started to go downhill.

We went from spending maybe an hour a day together to spending every… single… breathing… moment together. She managed to get another job (a remote one), so now not only did we live together, but we also worked together and went to the toilet together. OK, that's a joke – we had become codependent but not *that* codependent.

You're not meant to be around one other person all the time. I only just about like being around myself that much. And when the news is full of doom and you're stuck in your tiny little flat with only a tiny little patio for outside space, well… of course it's going to have an effect on your relationship. If it didn't then you would be a psychopath, and I'm happy to announce that neither Cat nor I are psychopaths. Yet… My money's on her. (Lol, joke. *Obviously* it's going to be me.)

……

Present day
It's been nearly two years since our fake online wedding, and those small seeds of doubt are now big-ass oak trees. There's only one person to blame: Walt – fucking – Disney.

Disney films (along with shows like *The L Word* and basically anything made in Hollywood) portray relationships as these perfect, all-consuming love adventures, filled with non-stop laughter, excitement and shagging. And any relationship that looks different to this insane codependent depiction of love is, clearly, not correct. At least, that's how I feel.

The beginning of my relationship with Cat was lovely… I was so excited to see her and I'd follow her into every room and pop little notes under the toilet door that read, 'Finish pooping already, I miss you'.

But then the butterflies stopped flapping, we stopped having sex as much and it wasn't as exciting, intense or all-consuming as it had been at the beginning. But all those bloody movies told me that it should have been!

Me: Should I still be getting butterflies?
Earl: Yes, but your butterflies have died and are now specks of dust.
Me: But I love her so much – maybe we just need to add something new into the relationship.
Wanda: Like a third person? You could be a thruple!
Me and Earl: No.
Wanda: A third person could do all the jobs that you two don't like doing, like cleaning the guinea pig cage, sorting out the bills or calling Cat's mother.
Me: We're still planning on moving to Edinburgh. Once we're there, everything will be better.
Earl: Yes, I'm sure the rain capital of the world will bring your relationship the joy it so very much needs…

Edinburgh is the answer to all my prayers – not that I pray, but if I did, Edinburgh would be the answer. The city is beautiful. It's full of character and friendly Scots and has a very sexy literary vibe about it. *However*, Edinburgh is also cold, full of bastard hills and 450 miles away from our flat in West Sussex. But, we plan to move there this year to start our new exciting life.

In my head, Edinburgh is going to solve everything – we'll have friends, we'll have jobs that we love, we'll go out and live life, we'll even get a dog and everything will be amazing again.

We've both managed to get jobs in Edinburgh that allow us to work remotely until we move (like I said before, I work in marketing, which means that I try to make people feel like they lack something in their life so that they'll part with their money in order to become more fulfilled. Yes, I hate me too).

We've lived in this small, boring town in West Sussex for four years now and it's slowly sucked the life out of me. We *have* to move to Edinburgh, otherwise I'm not sure my sanity (and therefore our relationship) will survive.

We've been trying to sell our flat for over a year, but it seems like we're only attracting Catholics because all of our buyers keep pulling out. We've had four buyers pull out in the last 10 months.

Is this a sign from the Universe? Are we failing to move because we aren't meant to be together? I can't imagine ever living without her, but since the pandemic has made our lives so small and miserable, I don't know anymore. I feel beyond stuck in a deep despair and I have a feeling that I'm dragging Cat down with me.

Earl: And there's only room in this pit for one of you.
Me: Exactly… Something has to change.
Earl: Well, this is apparently your year of 'transformation'.
Me: So I need to transform my mental health, my physical health *and* my relationship?
Earl: Or just stay stuck and wait for the sweet relief of death.
Me: No, that's no longer an option.
Wanda: Yay, choose life!!!
Me and Earl: Shut up, Wanda.

CHAPTER 3

WATCH OUT FOR THE ETERNAL THRUSH

It's now the second week of January and the new healthy me is going well. I've only consumed five chocolate bars, which is an 83 per cent improvement on the previous week. Yesterday, Cat treated us both to a float spa to help me get the mental health side of this transformation really rocking.

What the hell is a float spa? Well, it's like a yoga parlour, but instead of there being yoga mats in the middle of the room, there's a big-ass bathtub with a lid. This is what idiots like us pay £65 an hour to float about in – in the hope that we will emerge with meaning and purpose.

You could say that these float spas are just for morons who buy into all the 'self-care and wellbeing' bullshit. And you'd be right – if something even *hints* that it'll give me peace, love or serenity then I'm going to throw my money at it. Hence my cupboard at home that is rammed full of precious stones, mindfulness candles and things that tickle my chakras.

I went to the float spa to quieten my mind because my

biggest problem in life is that it never shuts up.

> **Earl:** You must overthink everything in absolute minute detail, otherwise you won't know how to progress in life.
> **Me:** But I'm not progressing in life.
> **Earl:** Well, you should probably think about why that is.
> **Me:** Because you won't let me.
> **Earl:** That's right, progression is pointless. Well done me.

When we first entered the spa (a basement flat in the middle of Brighton) the receptionist asked us to take our shoes and socks off. Oh God, not my socks as well, had I shaved my feet? Phew, I had. Sure, looking like a Mediterranean goddess is fantastic, but it does come with a lot of hair management.

After sipping on some disgusting ginger tea in the 'relaxation room' (a cupboard with a chair), we were escorted to our flotation rooms.

My flotation room was full of wires, hoses and a large noisy generator in the corner – you know, to really amplify the peace. The flotation tank (bath with a lid) sat huge in the middle of the room. It basically looked like a hippo's mouth but with water and a shitload of Epsom salts inside. The spa assistant wished me a happy float and left.

There are three rules that you have to follow while in the floaty tank – one, no weeing, two, no floaters (lolz) and three, although you're nice and relaxed, it's definitely not a good idea to have a fiddle with yourself, because the high concentration of Epsom salts will give you eternal thrush.

This wasn't my first time at a float spa. The previous session I had was a few years back and I found the entire thing quite boring. I just spent the whole hour swimming about and having fun opening and closing the lid.

'You really need to have quite a few sessions before it

SCREWED UP, SLIMMED DOWN

works in quietening the mind,' the spa assistant assured me. Oh great, do you accept credit card or shall I just get my wages paid directly into your account?

However, this time was different. After taking off all my clothes (please take a moment to picture me naked – gorgeous, I assure you), I stepped into the tub, floated myself into the middle and closed the lid. After three minutes the swishy wave sounds that were coming out of the speakers inside the tub stopped and the dim purple lights at the bottom of the tank went out. I was in total… dark… silence…

Earl: Sup, bitch.

Me: Not now, Earl. I'm quieting my mind and getting to the theta state.

Earl: Why does life suck so much?

Me: I'm not listening.

Earl: Thank God I keep you feeling stuck and dead inside, or you'd probably explode with all the emotion.

Me: Still not listening…

Earl: It's a shame that your friendship with Mel went balls up, isn't it? She became a bit of a dick after she lost weight.

Me: That's very true, she did change a lot. I hope I don't turn into a dick when I lose weight.

Earl: That'll never happen.

Me: Aw, thanks Earl.

Earl: Because you're never going to lose weight.

Me: …

Earl: Plus you're already a dick.

Me: Whatever.

Earl: I wonder if you should talk to Mel about how she's changed or just resent her from a distance until the friendship is well and truly fucked.

Me: Stop it, Earl, I'm not listening.

Earl: If you did tell her that you don't like the person she's turned into she'll probably hate you and block you on Facebook, and then it'll be really awkward 'cause she'll still be friends with Cat, and then she'll basically turn her against you. Although to be fair you're doing a pretty good job of that yourself.

An old therapist of mine used to comment on my incessant overthinking.

'Jenna, be more like a bricky,' he said to me on multiple occasions. Be more like a bricky? What, a wolf-whistling, beer-swilling misogynist? Naturally, I'm joking! That's an awful stereotype and definitely not a description of the only bricky I know. Clive… sort it out, mate.

But it's true, I do overthink *a lot*. But when you're as introverted as I am, you get good at thinking. You get good at just watching and listening and adding meaning to absolutely everything.

During university I had to write a dissertation on the film *The Hours* (the one where Nicole Kidman has a penis nose) and I got the best marks in my class on that dissertation because I went through that film with a fricking fine-tooth comb and described the meaning in every… single… little… thing. The use of the colour red? Oh, that has so much meaning – love, anger, passion, danger. But that's easy. What about the use of cutlery during the conversation between Alison Janey and Meryl Streep's characters? *Drowning* in meaning.

Unfortunately, I have kept this particular skill that I developed during my university days and I continue to apply it to everyday life. Everything anybody ever says or does or doesn't say or do has so much meaning. For example, if someone for some strange reason were to ask me to hang out but they crossed their legs while they said it, then do they *actually* want to hang out? Because their closed body language would suggest otherwise, so are they just asking me because they feel they have to? Obviously yes! And then what I'll do is look for signs to support my theory that they don't actually want to hang out and that will eventually turn into a self-fulfilling prophecy. It is *exhausting*.

> **Earl:** I wonder if these Epsom salts can go up your bum and give you bowel cancer.
> **Me:** …
> **Earl:** I wonder if the people at tennis hate you and wish you didn't play with them anymore.
> **Me:** …
> **Earl:** They must find you a bit annoying, I mean, you are really irritating and desperate.
> **Me:** …
> **Earl:** Jenna?
> **Me:** …
> **Earl:** Jennaaaaaaaaa?

Forty minutes after stepping into the flotation tank and going through everything that had ever happened and could ever possibly happen, my mind fell silent. No thoughts were coming, I was just present. I wasn't asleep, I was in the theta state and my mind was free. It was incredible.

This lasted for a good five minutes and only ended when the swishing sounds began to start up again and the purple lights came back on, signifying the end of the session.

Five minutes of pure freedom from my mind, at £65 an hour that works out to be £13 a minute – worth every bloody penny.

I meditate every other day, but I only do it for 10 minutes at a time because the capitalist society in which we live says I've got to work to earn money to pay for things like Nike trainers and MacBook Pros. So, I've never really got time to properly silence Earl quite like I did in the floaty tank.

Cat didn't really enjoy the float tank experience, she just found the whole thing a bit boring and has now vowed to

25

SCREWED UP, SLIMMED DOWN

never do it again. But would *I* do it again? Probably not, because although it shushed Earl up for a while, it was £65 for five minutes. I think the next time I've got a spare £65 to spend on my wellbeing, I'll get a massage and enjoy an hour of someone rubbing oil all over my gorgeous body rather than floating about in a bath where I spend three-quarters of the time wondering if I've been seriously robbed.

CHAPTER 4

INTRODUCING JENNA'S
FORM OF KETO

As someone who has the tendency to be codependent, I'm going to need something to help get me through the tough times during this transformation. So I've decided I'm going to start drinking again… No, but seriously, what I'm going to do is throw myself into my tennis. Tennis is good for my physical and mental health, so, during those times when Earl is overwhelming me that bit too much, I'm going to go and hit the shit out of a tennis ball instead.

I first discovered the game of tennis at university. Having previously grown up in a house where sport was banned from the TV due to my ex-stepdad being so obsessed with football that my mother went on to ban all sports from the house, I thought that sport was a) boring, b) pointless and, c) beneath me. It's not that I'm stuck up… it's just that I'd only ever known sport to be watched by lowlifes in the pub who'd smash pint glasses over each other's heads when their team scored. I jest, of course – those people are the salt of the earth.

But on one lonely afternoon between lectures I decided

that it might be a good idea to work off some of the cookies and Lambrini that I'd been bingeing on every night to stop myself from feeling lonely. So, I popped over to the gym and, as I started fannying about on the rowing machine, I began to watch my first ever bit of tennis that was being played on the TV in front of me.

It was Wimbledon, and it was utterly thrilling! It turned out that this silly little game of tennis was actually bloody amazing and after watching it for 25 minutes I was hooked (and absolutely shattered – seriously, 25 minutes on the rowing machine and I couldn't feel my arms for a fortnight).

From then on I watched tennis religiously, but I never thought of playing it because I thought that a) I was too fat, b) I was too shit and, c) it was only for rich snobs who could afford to join a tennis club.

Turns out I was wrong. Shit… I hate being wrong.

Having spent the first Covid lockdown playing tennis on the VR system that Cat and I played with for hours every day, I decided that I should get off my hairy, pimply bum and go and actually play it in real life. So, two years ago at the grand old age of 30, I picked up my first tennis racket and toddled along to a coaching session at a tennis club 35 minutes away, near Hove.

I was riddled with anxiety and fear because I thought that people would mock me and boo me out of the club. But actually the session was a lot of fun and no one booed me at all (not that I heard anyway). Sure, I didn't actually manage to make contact *with* the ball, but that's probably not an important part of the game.

'What do you think I need to work on?' I asked the coach.

'Everything,' she replied without a hint of humour.

Ah… I was rather hoping that I had a natural talent for tennis that I just hadn't tapped into yet. Apparently not. This was something I'd have to *actually* work on. Balls…

That was two years ago and I've been working on it

here and there, but since I started this transformation I've upped my tennis quite a bit. I now play twice a week and I am *thrilled* to announce that I am now marginally better than when I first started. So much so that last weekend I took my tennis to another level by attending a two-day tennis camp in the arse end of the world – Milton Keynes.

When I arrived on the Friday night, I popped by the little Tesco next to my hotel (it was an Ibis, so not really a 'hotel' but more of a squatting house with a receptionist). I browsed the aisles for something for dinner that didn't require any more effort than opening a wrapper. A meal deal it was! I bloody love a meal deal – a sandwich, a Coke *and* a chocolate bar? Thank you very much.

As I wandered to the till I noticed a sea of Easter eggs glaring back at me. Hello… Now, if you've ever had the advantage of meeting me (or disadvantage, depending on how you feel about me) then you'll know that I'm an absolute whore when it comes to Easter eggs. The chocolate, the taste, the thickness of the shell, the snap sound it makes when you break it apart – everything about them. God, I think I'm coming right now.

> **Wanda:** But what about the weight loss, Jenna? Let's get a banana for dessert instead! *Yeah, potassium!*
> **Earl:** Shut up Wanda, it's only Easter for four months of the year. Get the egg.

I got the egg. Sitting on my hotel bed I scoffed the meal deal down quickly before turning to the egg and… slowly… tenderly… unravelling it from its little tinfoil jacket. And, there it was, all gorgeous and smooth. *Beep beep*, my phone vibrated. *What? Not now, I'm having chocolate sex!*

It was my new friend, Louise, who I recently met at the tennis club.

'How's Milton Keynes?' Louise asked.

'Awful, I hear they're going to knock it down to build

slums,' I replied before returning to my egg.

Leaning back against the headboard with my legs outstretched in front of me, I laid the tinfoil on my knee and smashed the egg hard against it. I took the largest shard and put it in my mouth, every ounce of me melting like the chocolate on my tongue.

'What are you up to?' I asked Louise.

'Cooking dinner,' she replied.

'What are you having?'

'An omelette,' she replied. 'I'm really trying to lose four pounds.'

'Four pou— Four fucking pounds? Try four bloody stone, Louise!' I said out loud to myself as I ate more Easter egg.

'Are you doing anything special to lose four pounds?' I asked.

'Keto,' she replied.

What the hell on God's green earth is bloody keto? I mean, sure, I've heard and seen the word before, but like with the nutritional value on my food, I'd completely ignored it. I put the Easter egg down and opened up Google.

'What is keto?' I asked.

Keto is a high-fat, low-carb diet that forces the body to burn fat rather than carbohydrates. Brilliant, I've got loads of fat to burn. I continued to research…

The basic premise of keto is to only have 50 grams of carbohydrates a day. The rest of your food should come from protein and a lot of fat. Like, a *lot* of fat. Unfortunately, not the delicious saturated fat like in the Easter egg I had nearly finished, but in foods like avocados, cheese, nuts, eggs (again, not the Easter kind) and meat.

At first, I was sceptical – wasn't this basically the Atkins diet? And didn't Mr Atkins die of his own diet? A lot like the inventor of the Segway died on a Segway (that was falling off a cliff).

Earl: I wonder if you're going to die of your own bad jokes?

I opened up the food tracking app where I'd begun to record everything that I eat on a daily basis to really keep an eye on what I'm consuming. (Turns out it's a lot... shit, do I really have that many snacks in one day?)

The app told me that I roughly consume 278 grams of carbohydrates a day and no, that doesn't include the Easter egg.

'Right, well, I'm not going to go down to 50 then, am I?' I said to myself with a mouth full of chocolate. I planned to cut down my carbs by half, and then see how I got on. I also planned to stop buying crap from the shop. I mean, come on – a meal deal and an Easter egg for dinner? What am I, 10 years old? No, I'm a 16-stone, grown-ass 32-year-old woman who should know better...

Also, it was the third week of January and I'd only lost three pounds, and three pounds in the first month of the year that Jenna gets super sexy and fit is *not* enough.

Mentally, the first few weeks of my transformation had gone quite well. I'd organised things to get myself out of my flat – hence the tennis weekend in slumland Milton Keynes. I'd also been meditating *every* day and trying my best not to let my work overwhelm me by going out on walks during my lunch break rather than sitting and playing Candy Crush on the sofa.

But no matter how much I thought I was doing better mentally, the bingeing of chocolate on my own in a hotel room is not the sign of a well-balanced individual. I was clearly repressing some feelings somewhere. The heavy black ball of sadness that sits in the pit of my stomach is still very much there, no matter how much I try to cover it up with refined sugar. That niggling voice of doom just won't sod off.

SCREWED UP, SLIMMED DOWN

Earl: I'll always be here.
Me: Piss off, dickhead.
Earl: That's so rude, no wonder you have no friends.

The tennis weekend was so much fun. Earl never joins me at tennis because I'm too busy trying to chase the ball and not thump it into the net to allow him into my mind.

'Are you serving ice cream?' the coach asked me as I practised my serve.

'Pardon?'

'Because that was one soft serve.' Oh, a pun, excellent. 'Put some welly into it. Really throw your racket,' he said.

'Like this?' I asked, pedantically, before hammering down the hardest serve I could, which inevitably made the ball go straight into the net and the racket go sliding out of my hand.

'Yeah, but over the net,' he laughed. 'And try to keep hold of the racket.' Ahh, tennis bantz… very good.

I did, however, do an excellent one-handed backhand passing shot down the line, but as the ball left my strings I slipped and fell like a sack of shit. Still, whatever wins the point.

When I arrived back home I immediately did an online shop and filled my basket with avocados, eggs (*no, not the chocolate kind, FFS*), full-fat cheese, almond milk, protein shakes and ice packs for my lower back (stupid tennis, making me fall on my arse in front of everyone and flaring up my sciatica).

I learnt three very important things in Milton Keynes – the first one being that I don't like Milton Keynes and I don't ever plan to go back there. The second one is that I needed a shiny new very expensive tennis racket because, compared to the other people at the tennis weekend, mine looked like something from prehistoric times. And thirdly, it was really eye-opening to see just how many carbs there are in things that you don't expect there to be carbs in. Obviously, bread is full of carbs (I'm not as stupid as I look), but there's also a lot in sweetcorn, tomatoes and even oat milk. Oat milk is made from oats (duh) which is apparently *full* of carbs. Who knew? Apparently everyone… OK, maybe I am as stupid as I look.

The first few days of trying keto went well. I managed to keep the carbs down to just 120 grams, which is hard because carbs taste amazing and I want all the carbs all the time. But at least I'm allowed cheese. Mmmm… cheese.

Keto is going to be my new way of life. But not the full keto because 50 grams of carbs a day is absolute bullshit. I'm going to do 'Jenna's form of keto'. What's Jenna's form of keto? Well, it's keto but with more carbs. I've been doing it for a week now and I've already dropped three pounds.

God, I'm going to get so sexy.

CHAPTER 5

HYPNOTHERAPY BY THE SEX POOL

February

I've dabbled in quite a few therapies throughout my life, including but not limited to psychotherapy, psychodynamic therapy, cognitive analytical therapy, humanistic therapy, cognitive behaviour therapy and therapy therapy, but I've *never* tried hypnotherapy. So today, I popped along to my first session.

To say that I had low expectations would be a lie. I expected the venue to be a dark dinky cave that would be drowning in candles, fairy lights and incense sticks. The hypnotherapist would be barefoot, sitting on a homemade cushion and wearing a long tie-dye dress, looking batshit kooky. She'd get out her pocket watch, put me in a trance, do a little spell, a few chants, maybe scream a bit and then BOOM! I'd emerge fully healed and cured of all mental health issues forever and ever, amen.

It wasn't like that.

I arrived at the venue, a posh little clinic hidden in the depths of the West Sussex countryside, and was greeted by a short, grey-haired woman in a twinset wearing sensible shoes. Not a single candle in sight.

SCREWED UP, SLIMMED DOWN

'So, why have you come to hypnotherapy?' she asked, sitting down opposite me and placing her hands neatly in her lap.

'I've been unhappy in my life for quite a long time.'

'What's making you unhappy?'

'How long have you got?' I joked.

'We've got 50 minutes,' she replied. If I wanted to make her laugh I was clearly going to have to work harder.

I told her about my panic attacks, my childhood and how my negative outlook on life affects everything and makes me feel like a depressed piece of poop.

'What do you think your life would be like if you didn't have depression?' she asked. I opened my mouth to reply and then closed it again. Shit. What *would* my life be like if I didn't have depression?

I tried to imagine what it would look like. It looked fantastic, but it looked impossible.

'It would be light,' I replied, smiling. 'I'd feel happier, less burdened by life and I'd be myself. My authentic self who isn't so self-conscious and negative. I'd also enjoy things more and I wouldn't keep feeling sad because they're going to end.'

Earl: I have a suggestion.

Me: Oh God.

Earl: If you don't start things then they can't end, if they can't end, then you can't feel sad about them. Ergo, just don't bother starting anything.

I told the hypnotherapist about my lack of self-esteem, my shockingly low confidence and my non-existent self-worth.

'I don't feel worthy enough to make friends. I think they'll realise that I'm just a waste of space, they'll get bored of me and then I'll feel rejected and shit and I'll just end up alone again,' I told her. Sorry, dear reader, could you not play that violin so loudly, please? The strings go right through my sinuses.

'What's going to happen now is I'm going to walk you through some breathing exercises to calm your mind and centre yourself, and eventually you'll enter the trance,' she said, taking off her glasses and putting them on the cabinet beside her.

Once I was in the trance she told me to go to a happy place in my mind. I pictured the private plunge pool outside the villa that Cat and I had stayed at in Bali for my 30th birthday a few years ago. The pool was warm, peaceful and surrounded by huge exotic plants. It was the most luxurious place I've ever had sex. Hey, don't be judging me, you'd do the same if you had your own pool.

'Now, I want you to imagine you're sitting on a chair in your happy place and opposite you is an old TV monitor. On the TV is a scenario from your past. Pick a scene from an event that made you feel like you weren't worthy.' Gosh, which one to pick… 'I now want you to imagine that the scene is playing on the TV.'

I pictured the scene:

Me in the school playground surrounded by a group of twats, or '10-year-old boys' if you want to call them that.

'Oi, Jenna, you bloke!' one of them shouted.

'I'm not a bloke!' I yelled back.

'I'm not a bloke,' one of them mocked me, but in a deeper lower voice. 'Yeah, well, how come you got hairier legs than my dad?'

'Stop it,' I pleaded.

'Aww, stop it,' they mocked some more. 'Where's your friends, Jenna?'

'Leave me alone.'

'Who would want to be friends with you anyway? You fat bloke,' the leader of the pack said, making all the other boys burst into a fit of laughter. I pushed my way out of the circle that they'd made around me and ran to the toilet, where I cried until the end of time.

'Now imagine your spirit is coming out of your body

and is standing next to the TV as the scene plays out.'

I imagined my spirit coming out of my body and walking over to stand next to the TV. 'Now, play the scene again, but this time I want your spirit to jump into the scene.'

OK…

While my spirit was in the scene, the other me was still sitting in the chair by the pool holding the remote control and watching it play out.

She then told me to rewind the scene and play it again. 'But this time I want you to play it back at double speed,' she said. I played it back at double speed. The boys' voices were now higher and it made them sound silly. 'And now play it back at half the speed.' Their voices were now slow, low and made them sound even dumber (as if that was possible).

I continued to rewind the scene and play it back while messing about with the speed, the pitch of their voices and even adding a funny soundtrack. What this did was change how I felt about the memory and therefore change how it affected me. Because now, this bitch (me) is in charge and I'm not giving those twatty little 10-year-old boys the power over me anymore.

We did this technique with two other situations in my life that have not only contributed to my lack of self-worth but also helped instil my fundamental belief that a) I'm only wanted by people if I'm useful to them in some way, and b) if I don't do what other people want me to do, then they won't love me anymore. Love is transactional.

At the end of the last scene the hypnotherapist told me to take the DVDs out of the TV monitor, put them in their DVD box and then do whatever I wanted with them. I imagined throwing them up high and then shooting them out of the air like I was clay-pigeon shooting.

The TV monitor then disappeared and turned into a big super cinema system and future me was on the screen. Future Jenna was dancing and smiling at me, her happiness shining brightly in her face.

'Everything is going to be OK, my love,' future Jenna said to me as she stopped dancing. 'You will find purpose, you will find hope and although things are tough now, they *will* get better, I promise.' Future me then reached out of the screen and pressed a green precious stone into the middle of my chest. A feeling of hope, love and happiness flooded through me.

A tear ran down my face and I sat with this warm feeling until the hypnotherapist brought me back into the room.

'I am reborn!' I announced to Cat when I got home.

'How was it?' she asked.

'It was really bloody good, although she didn't have a pocket watch, that was a bit of a let-down. But there were three Jennas, well, four if you include me and I was watching my childhood play out next to the pool we had sex in in Bali.'

'What?'

'I think I'll go again.'

CHAPTER 6

WE ARE THE FRUITCAKES OF OUR MOTHER'S LOIN

Did I mention that my brother is also a big gay? Sorry, it must have totally slipped my mind, what with gay men just being a bunch of guys who can't get a woman. (That's a joke, keep your tiaras on.)

Even though my big idiot brother is five years older than me, I came out nine years before him (it's the only thing that I've managed to beat him on). When my brother was young he used to push a pram around the garden and our grandma told my mum that if she let him do that then he would end up gay. Well, my granny turned out to be quite the fortune teller, didn't she?

Though I don't think the pram-pushing had anything to do with him being gay. Just like me playing with a toolbox instead of dollies didn't turn me into a lesbian. Sure, it was certainly a sign, but not the root cause.

The best bit about having a gay brother is when I tell other people that both me and him are gay, and then I get to watch their reaction as they try not to look shocked or immediately start thinking that our parents did something wrong.

Unfortunately, our parents *did* do something wrong because my brother turned out to be a big Tory-voting capitalist butthead who doesn't use his indicator. But then they *did* do something right with me, because I turned out to be a bunny-hugging absolute saint who uses her indicator at every opportunity.

Earl: Have you blocked each other on Facebook?
Me: No.
Earl: Do you still send each other birthday cards?
Me: Yes.
Earl: If he was on fire, would you piss on him?
Me: Most probably.
Earl: Then your relationship is better than some siblings.
Me: Thanks, Earl. Why so positive?
Earl: I don't know. I will now restart and hope that my normal negative attitude recommences.

Over the past few years I've been slowly learning to ignore my brother when he goes off on one of his silly rants. For example, here's one I had the privilege of hearing after the last Covid lockdown.

'Look at all these berks still wearing masks,' he said, pointing to the people standing at the bus stop as we drove past them. 'All that Covid rubbish is over, get those masks off!'

'People are still catching it,' I said.

'Let's just all crack on, forget all this Covid this, Covid that.'

'Well, at least there's no lockdowns or restrictions anymore.'

'What a load of old shit that was. I can't believe they closed the gyms! It's not us healthy young people dying of it…'

SCREWED UP, SLIMMED DOWN

Wanda: Careful, Jenna. He's just trying to get a reaction out of you.

I took a deep breath and just rolled my eyes. I love my brother very much, but our relationship works much better when instead of trying to reason with him, I just sit back and take the moral high ground.

Family though, am I right? Can't live with them, and why the hell would you want to? But then there are people who get a big family plot in the graveyard so that they can all be together in death as well. Bizarre!

Dear family, I am joking of course, in fact, I would *love* for our earthly remains to all be mixed together so we can be united for all of eternity.

My dad left when I was two years old, so it was just my mum, brother and me left in the family home.

We got on well when we were younger, my brother and I especially. We played a lot and were silly, constantly trying to make each other laugh. But the older we got, the more we changed and became our own people, growing further apart. I no longer wanted to be the little sister that was bossed about and made fun of by her older brother. And my brother was suddenly too old and cool to hang out with his annoying little sister.

There have been times over the past few years where spending time with my family has been difficult, because we're such different people now – our morals, our values, just everything is different. However, thanks to all the hard work I'd been doing recently on my zen-ness (basically reading Eckhart Tolle and pausing to breathe before responding to anything that might trigger me), I'm able to spend more and more time with my family without wanting to go home and put my head in the oven (naturally, I jest).

Last week Cat and I were invited to stay with my brother and his husband for the weekend. So on Friday night we packed up the car and made our way down to their house in Dorset.

Bizarrely, Cat doesn't get as panicky as I do when she's hanging out with my family, but of course, it's lovely to see *other people* deal with *their* family. God, it's so entertaining. To see the dynamic, the undertones, the subtle passive-aggressive digs and general 'dance' that happens within a family that isn't yours (or at least isn't yours by blood) is one of life's great gifts. But to deal with your *own* family… oh, pure hell.

'If you start to get anxious, just give me a look and we can leave,' Cat said as we pulled up outside my brother's house.

For the past year, I've been suffering from bad panic attacks. I've had bouts of anxiety for a few years, but these new terrifying panic attacks are a whole other kettle of petrified fish.

The panic attacks are normally focused around becoming terminally ill, losing Cat or having a lonely and young death. You know, the trivial stuff. During an attack I get extremely flustered, sweaty, short of breath and unable to do anything other than cry, sweat and manically shake my head while muttering, 'I can't do this. I can't do this. I can't do this.'

But they come out of NOWHERE. I have *no idea* what triggers them. So, I never know when one of the bastards is going to pop its stupid head up.

'Have you done any more of your scrapbook yet?' Cat asked, knowing full well that I hadn't.

My scrapbook is a really lovely tan book; however, it is also a really *empty* tan book that's just been waiting for me to stick pictures and memories inside it so that when the thoughts of death, illness and despair begin to flood me, I have something to look at to remind me that my life is good, has been worth living and continues to be worth living.

I have not stuck a single memory in the scrapbook.

SCREWED UP, SLIMMED DOWN

Why? Well, because that would require effort and printer ink, neither of which I have. Also, when I'm not having a panic attack I don't want to be thinking about my panic attacks, and doing a scrapbook to help me during a panic attack is *technically* panic-attack related.

'No. But I will!' I said, popping the last grape into my mouth before getting out of the car. (My car snacks have seriously improved, by the way – no more Mini Rolls and Party Rings. Just grapes and the occasional teeny tiny chocolate bar.)

My brother, his husband, Cat and I all went out for a meal in a rather expensive restaurant in Bournemouth, booked by my brother because apparently he's now 'too posh' to go anywhere that could be referred to as 'mildly affordable'.

After the dinner we returned to my brother's house and all went to bed, but then BAM! – the demons arrived. Where the fuck had they come from? Who the hell knows? Not me… The only pattern in my panic attacks is that they mainly happen at night. The demons make me feel so horrendous that they make Earl look like a box of fluffy kittens.

Earl: Meow.

'I can feel the panic coming up, babe,' I said to Cat as we got into the little double bed in my brother's attic room.

'It's OK. Just breathe,' she said, putting a comforting hand on my chest. 'What's it focusing on?'

'I just feel all this doom and darkness. I keep thinking about death and how everything is bad and we're all going to die – and what if I die tonight? I haven't done what I wanted. I haven't lived yet. I just feel so scared. I can't do this. I can't do this. I can't do this,' I said, sitting up in the bed. The panic was rising, the dark clouds were engulfing, the panic attack was here.

SCREWED UP, SLIMMED DOWN

'You're not going to die tonight. Everything is OK, darling. Just concentrate on your breath, in and out,' Cat said calmly as she shuffled up in the bed and rubbed my arm reassuringly.

'But you don't know that,' I tried to argue with her. 'What if I get cancer next week and only have a few weeks left to live? What if we break up and I don't have you here and I have to do life without you? Everything just feels so awful, babe, I can't do this anymore.'

'In… and… out…' she continued. 'Long and deep. In… and… out…'

If you've never had a panic attack, then the only way I can best describe it to you is imagine that you're a little fish in a tank. The water is clear and you're just happily swimming about like the little fish you are, but then suddenly a huge dollop of ink is plopped into the water and slowly the once clear water turns dark and the ink swishes about and pollutes everything in the tank and you're surrounded by complete darkness. You try to find a way out, but there is no way out because you're in a tank and the ink is poison so you just choke and die because you're a fucking fish and the world is shit.

Earl: Jesus, that's a bit dark, isn't it?

'Take a propranolol, darling,' Cat said as she handed me the packet of prescription drugs. I took one with some water and continued to just focus on my breathing while I waited for the panic to pass.

Propranolol is a beta blocker, which helps block the effects of the adrenaline and noradrenaline (the two chemicals released during a panic attack) that cause me to sweat, shake and make my heart race quicker than when I see a picture of Kate Winslet.

Slowly but surely the panic subsided enough for me to sob my way to sleep in Cat's tight embrace.

Why does this keep happening? How am I ever going

to get rid of these panic attacks? I just want to feel normal again.

Thank God Cat is here to save me.

CHAPTER 7

EVERYTHING IS OK, DON'T PANIC!

It's been a week since we stayed at my brother's house and I can still feel the aftereffects of the panic attack.

I feel stuck. I feel burdened, with life, with the problems in my relationship, with my heavy belly and with the fact that this week I had to go up to Edinburgh for a work meeting *despite* the fact that everyone in the company has bloody Zoom. Not that I don't *love* going up to visit the city that I will soon be calling home, it's just the work bollocks that I don't like.

I'm having anxiety and doubts about everything in my life, *plus* I'm ovulating, which turns me into a hormonal psycho and the lens through which I normally view life turns into one of those weird kaleidoscope toys that I had as a child. Without being too dramatic, NOTHING MAKES SENSE AND EVERYTHING IS SHIT.

Once the meeting, the networking and the anxiety attacks in the hotel were over, I made my way back to Edinburgh airport to fly back down to London. The tram ride from the city centre to the airport took me through a vast array of neighbourhoods.

SCREWED UP, SLIMMED DOWN

I have meticulously studied these neighbourhoods using an online deprivation map that tells me whether an area is good enough for the likes of me (a posh-sounding southern English snob). I just type in the name of the area and it tells me on a scale of blue to red (blue being good, red being bad, anything to do with political parties? Hmmm, coincidence, I'm sure) whether the area is good or bad depending on the employment, education and crime rate.

Although property in Edinburgh is cheaper than in the south of England, it's still pretty pricy. So, my filtering system for areas where we should look for houses is 'stabby enough that we can afford to live there, but not so stabby that we'll actually get stabbed'. And last year we found the perfect area and the perfect house. But that was before our 900th buyer pulled out and we ended up losing that house. Those damn Catholics!

When I arrived at Edinburgh airport I made my way through security and began the walk to my gate. But as I started walking, my heart started to beat faster, the back of my neck started to get hot and I felt the panic begin to rise from my stomach. It made its way up through my torso, up through my tight chest, into my head and finally reached my mind.

And that's when it took over.

'Oh God, no, not now, it's OK, it's OK,' I muttered to myself as I tried my best to keep walking towards the gate.

Within seconds I was flooded with the worst panic I have ever felt. I couldn't even think straight (enter lesbian joke here). I couldn't even force myself to stop walking and get a propranolol from my bag. I needed Cat.

Me: What's happening???
Earl: I don't know! This has got nothing to do with me.
Me: Then where is it coming from? What am I panicking about?

47

SCREWED UP, SLIMMED DOWN

Earl: I mean, there's *so much* to panic about: war, disease, the entire annihilation of the human race in a few billion years. But this panic attack specifically? Not got a scoob, mate.
Me: I can't do this…
Earl: Oooo, hang on, I know! Maybe you're panicking because you're in Edinburgh, which is meant to make everything all shiny and fabulous, and you're just realising that maybe it's not the answer to your problems because you're still going to take your mind with you?
Me: WHAT?!
Earl: Just a guess.

To the left of me was a wall of glass windows looking out onto the runway. I normally like to stare out of these windows and imagine what wonderful and exotic countries the planes might take me to. But I couldn't this time. I couldn't do anything but stare at my feet.

'I can't do this. Oh God. Oh God. I can't do this.' The panic was getting so intense that I felt like I was seconds away from screaming out in a hysterical fit. (Aren't we all just seconds away from becoming that absolute nutter that we see shouting at themselves in the park?) I felt like I was going to die.

Wanda: Just look at your feet, Jenna. One step at a time. Right leg. Left leg. Right leg. Left leg. That's all you need to do, just walk.

I continued to walk, head down, staring at my feet. I couldn't even focus on my breath, that was too hard, but I *could* focus on the steps my feet were taking.

Wanda: This will pass. It's OK. Just look at your feet.

When I arrived at my gate I stopped and slid down the

wall next to the vending machine, the hot tears pouring down my face. I've never been so scared in all my life. Nor have I ever had such a large audience for a panic attack – seriously, people really do love to have a good look. But to be fair, I was just about to be on a plane with these people so naturally they had an interest in the current state of my mental wellbeing.

I eventually managed to reach into my bag and pop a propranolol which calmed me down enough that by the time the plane took off I was able to focus on my breathing and distract myself with Candy Crush. In future, I must remember to keep my propranolol in my pocket, for the next panic attack. This is my life at the moment, from one panic attack to the next.

CHAPTER 8

I AM A PRETTY LITTLE FLOWER

March

My first hypnotherapy appointment went so well that I thought I'd go for a second session. I considered using the session to help me work on my weight-loss shizz, but actually that was going quite well since I started doing 'Jenna's form of keto', plus there's a more pressing condition that I want help with. It's called 'the grass is always bloody greener wherever I'm not' syndrome and I've had it for decades.

Basically, I'm always unhappy with what I have and what I don't have is the only thing that will make me happy.

For example: I'll be happy once we move to Edinburgh, once I have a better job, have some friends, become thin and don't live in a patriarchal capitalist society that destroys our souls. But *actually*... do I truly believe that now? I'm not so sure. I also want to work on my inability to say yes. Well, Earl's inability.

Me: Do I want to go on holiday?

SCREWED UP, SLIMMED DOWN

Earl: No.
Me: Do I want to have sex?
Earl: No.
Me: Do I want to do anything meaningful in my life?
Earl: No. Why would you want to?
Me: So that I can make my short time on earth worth living.
Earl: No.
Me: Do I want to eat Easter eggs until the pain goes away?
Earl: Is that a trick question?

But I *do* want to go on holiday, have sex, do something meaningful and eat Easter eggs until the pain goes away and, yes, all at the same time would be fantastic. It would be like recreating some of the dreams I've had.

I get this particular fondness for saying 'no' to everything from my dad. He says no to every invitation; my mum, however, would go to the opening of an envelope. But I'm like my dad: covered in hair and an expert at saying no.

So, this week during my second session I told the hypnotherapist about my issues with saying yes and never being happy with what I have.

Once I'd finished wanging on, we went through the breathing exercises like before and then I went deep into the trance.

She told me to imagine that I was a little seed in some soil, and I watched as I grew roots and a stem and then, finally, some flowers. Beautiful, big colourful flowers. She then took me down a road within the trance (was I still a flower? Was I a walking flower? No, I think I'd gone back to being a human again at this point) and she told me to focus just on the walking, not on what was coming up further in the distance.

'There's a speed bump ahead, but we're not at it yet, so just focus on your current steps and go with the flow. We will deal with the speed bump when we get to it.'

I could see what she was doing. Me being a little seed that grew into a pretty little flower was her trying to make me feel happy with where I was right now, to feel grounded and rooted. And the speed bumps in the road of life? Well, I've always had a tendency to worry about problems down the road rather than enjoy where I am right now.

For example, when we first arrived at that private villa in Bali I was elated, and then very very soon afterwards I was sad because I knew that we'd have to leave in a week's time. This just ruins everything for me – I can't enjoy things knowing that they will end. But this is something I hope hypnotherapy can help me with. Yes, this extremely fun holiday/night out/shagging session will end, but I can enjoy it right now.

All in all the hypnotherapy has definitely been helping me. Sure, it's not a solution on its own, but in conjunction with exercise, meditation and all the chakra stones that I've bought off Etsy, I can definitely feel something changing within me.

CHAPTER 9

HOVE, ACTUALLY…

Cat and I have both been having anxiety this week. For me it's about the relationship, and for her it's about me having anxiety about the relationship. What a right pair of hot young things we are. So not only do I have all the anxiety about the relationship, but now I also have all the guilt because it's affecting Cat.

> **Earl:** What an excellent girlfriend you are…
> **Me:** Tell me about it.
> **Earl:** Maybe you should just put everyone out of their misery and go and be on your own like the spinster hermit you're destined to be.
> **Me:** Thanks for the support, Earl.
> **Earl:** Anytime.

We've got a new buyer for our flat and it seems like this one is actually not planning on pulling out #win. But, does moving to Edinburgh still feel right? Er, that'll be a big fat no.

'You'll take your problems with you,' numerous

SCREWED UP, SLIMMED DOWN

(un)helpful family members have said to both Cat and I. And although I'd absolutely HATE for them to be right, I think they might be…

Bollocks.

There's a part of me, deep down within my flabby belly, that knows that Edinburgh won't fix everything. Our lives won't suddenly change because we've moved location. I won't suddenly be this confident, self-assured woman who finds it easy to make friends, who suddenly enjoys working and has a sunny disposition. And how will putting our relationship in a colder, wetter climate make it suddenly better?

If we did move to bonnie Scotland, things might seem better for a few months, though slowly but surely the tedium and dread of everyday life will creep its way back in.

'Darling, I think we should stay in Sussex,' I said to Cat today after a lot of consideration. 'Obviously, we don't want to stay here in Haywards Heath and we need to get out of this flat. Maybe we should move into rented down near Hove, and really work on us,' I continued. Haywards Heath, for those fortunate enough not to have been here, is a little commuter town in West Sussex which is good for commuting and… that's about it.

As for our flat, well, since the pandemic hit it has become more like a prison than a home. Every time we go out we dread coming back, but when we *are* in the flat, we feel like we can't leave.

'But I want to move to Edinburgh,' she said.

'I do too, but I don't think we're in the right place right now to start our new exciting life. What with my doubts and panic attacks and your anxiety, I don't think our relationship would survive the move,' I said, rubbing her leg affectionately.

We've lived in Haywards Heath for four years and it's

only in the last year after joining the tennis club near Hove that I've actually started to make a little life for myself down here. I have a hobby now, I'm making friends at the tennis club… sure, we haven't socialised after tennis yet (baby steps) but I've started growing roots down here (looks like the hypnotherapist and her little seed trance thing has already begun to work) and I don't want to leave the life that's taken me four bloody years to make.

Also, I don't know anyone in Edinburgh. Cat knows a few people and has family in Scotland, but I have no one. Apart from Wanda and Earl of course, but they're about as helpful as a condom machine in the Vatican.

Me: Will moving to Edinburgh solve my problems?
Earl & Wanda: No.
Me: What the hell? Since when did you two form an allegiance?
Wanda: You must find the change within yourself, Jenna.
Earl: Eugh, bore off. Our allegiance is now over.

'I just don't know if it's the big shiny answer to our problems right now. We need to get out of this flat, but I think we need to pause on Edinburgh, until we're, well, *I'm* in a better place,' I said.

'Yeah, I know what you mean,' Cat said. 'I've been thinking something similar. Also, we both hate the jobs we've got in Edinburgh and that's kind of tainted the place.' I nodded. Both mine and Cat's Edinburgh jobs hadn't turned out to be the fantastic new happy jobs, like we'd hoped. WHAT A SHOCKER!

Cat had been working for a startup that thinks it's going to be the next Amazon (aka, the CEO is a psycho who works everyone into the ground) and my marketing job is… well, it's marketing. 'OK, let's go into rented somewhere down near Hove, work on us for a year and then see where we are.'

SCREWED UP, SLIMMED DOWN

'Sounds good,' I said, smiling, before leaning in to give her a kiss on the lips.

God, I hope this works out.

CHAPTER 10

TAKING LIFE ONE ANTIDEPRESSANT AT A TIME

I've been on antidepressants for 14 years and I feel like they no longer have any effect on me; in fact, I think that an erect penis would have more of an effect on me, which is not something I ever thought I'd write. So, last year I tried to come off them.

I started taking antidepressants in 2008 when I was 18 years old and getting over a period of unrequited love, which if you've never experienced it, is quite terrific. God, what a feeling… I had also been going through a series of horrendous arguments with my mum that resulted in me running away from my home in Devon every other weekend. Sometimes I'd even get as far as Reading before having to get the train back home with my tail between my legs.

During that time I was also an emo; my clothes, hair and soul were all blacker than a sombre raven flapping about in an oil spill. I also couldn't really bring myself to trust anyone else so I isolated myself, making zero effort to make friends with the other kids.

57

Looking back now, I realise that I didn't need antidepressants. I needed a puppy, some friends and some more upbeat music to listen to. (I still very much need those things.)

During those angsty teenage years I went to see a therapist a couple of times, but I wasn't a big fan of talking (and I hear that's quite an important part of therapy) so it didn't help much.

My mum, who is a big fan of tablets (seriously, if she could take a tablet that turns her fingernails different colours so that she doesn't have to paint them, she would take it) was extremely concerned when she saw that the therapy wasn't working (what with me being mute during the sessions), so instead she encouraged me to go to the doctor and get some antidepressants. She'd been on them herself in the past and apparently she'd experienced great things, so she thought they would work for me as well.

With the amount of reluctance that only a teenager can achieve, 18-year-old Jenna made a doctor's appointment and went to the surgery to ask for antidepressants.

'Just tell them that you want antidepressants and they'll give them to you,' my mum had told me before I'd left the house, and she wasn't wrong. As soon as I got into the doctor's office and sat my pimply teenage arse on the chair I told the doctor that I needed antidepressants, to which he asked me a few 'qualifying questions':

'How is college?'

'Shit.'

'Do you have many friends?'

'No.'

'What do you do after college?'

'Eat.'

'Do you feel sad, hopeless or empty?'

'Yes.'

'Do you find it hard to find pleasure in activities you used to enjoy?'

'The last thing I enjoyed was putting square pegs into

round holes as a baby, but even that got tedious.'

'Are you having trouble sleeping?'

'No, the harrowing screams in my head are actually a sweet lullaby.'

'Have you had thoughts about harming yourself or others?'

'Others.'

'Lastly, if you were to eat yourself, would you double in size or disappear altogether?'

'Hopefully the latter.'

Ten minutes later I walked out of the doctor's office with a prescription for 20mg of happy pills. The doctor had assured me that although they would take a good few weeks to have any effect, they would start to make me feel better eventually.

And sure, they did make me feel better. But only a bit... You know how you feel better when the gun pointing at your head is suddenly pointing at your leg instead? It was like that. Even though the medication softens the edges of my depression, it also takes away my sex drive, my sense of joy, and makes me feel numb. So, after 14 years of taking those little pills, last year I decided to start coming off them to see what life was like without antidepressants.

When I told my mum this she had a few concerns.

'Why?'

'Are you fine now?'

'You don't seem fine.'

'Why don't you just change the type of medication?'

'Why don't you just go on a higher dose?'

'What if things get bad again?'

'Why don't you just stay on them?'

'So-and-so from *Loose Women* has been on them for years and they'll be on them for the rest of their life, so why can't you?'

I'd attempted to come off antidepressants twice before, but both times were Horrendous with a capital H. Let's cut back to one of those times:

Me: I feel a bit anxious.
Earl: Only a bit? Allow me to change this…
10 seconds later
Me: THE WORLD IS AWFUL AND I'M GOING TO KILL MYSELF BY JUMPING OFF TOWER BRIDGE!
Earl: Don't jump off Tower Bridge, silly, jump off London Bridge – that way you'll get to see Tower Bridge on the way down. Everyone knows it's the nicer of the two bridges.

I'd get myself into such a state that all I'd want to do is quit my job, run away and pull all my hair out. The anxiety attacks, panic and utter despair were overwhelming and I wasn't able to cope, so I always had to go back on the medication.

I promised Cat that this time was going to be different. She's always been great at putting up with my mental fuggery (she'll just listen, say it's OK and then hug me), but I do realise that she must have a breaking point. I haven't found it yet, but surely she has one. Unless I've found the only person without one… Score!

Sadly, however, last year after three months of no antidepressants (after tapering off them over the course of seven months) I fell into a deeper, darker depression. One where I couldn't stop crying in the bath on the morning of my brother's wedding. Over what? I hear you ask. I DON'T KNOW, MY SUBCONSCIOUS DOESN'T TELL ME! I was just full of such sadness and despair. So, now his wedding photos are full of happy smiling family members and me, his weird younger sister with eyes more swollen than a bloated frog.

I had gotten what I wanted, to feel things again, but unfortunately I was feeling *all* of the things, *all* of the time.

I've been back on 50mg of Sertraline for six months

now. One day I'll come off them, but today is not that day. And that's OK.

I mean, it's not, because it proves my mother right, but still…

CHAPTER 11

HAS MY LONELINESS PEAKED YET?

April

Like the rest of the Sussex population, Cat and I popped to Brighton beach last week on the hottest day of the year so far (a sweltering 14 degrees Celsius). We went equipped with our yoga mats (to minimise the number of pebbles that went up our arses), our towels and our essential beach provisions, aka our sea shoes, a meal deal (a healthier version, of course, and no Easter egg this time) and numerous vegetarian picnic food items that look like, taste like, and have the nutritional content of... cardboard.

As I scoffed my sandwich (brown bread, yes, it's carbs but it's also fibre, your girl is backed up again), I looked around and watched as all the groups of students, gays and druggies around us laughed, yelled and generally expelled noises from the holes in their faces. Basically, they were having fun with their friends.

'I wish we had friends,' Cat said, breaking my train of thought, my train of thought being 'I wish we had friends.'

'Me too...' I replied with a sad smile. Everyone else seemed to be in a group of at least four people, either with

SCREWED UP, SLIMMED DOWN

a BBQ sitting in the middle of them or a little mountain of empty beer bottles that they were going to leave behind. But Cat and I just sat on our own, with our cardboard picnic.

I mean, we had each other and that *of course* is enough, but also sometimes it isn't. It's not good to put all your vegan Scotch eggs into one biodegradable basket.

Throughout my life I've always been pretty lonely and isolated, but Cat, being a jolly extroverted Dundonian, is used to having a lot of friends. But since she started living down in the south of England her friendship group has got smaller and smaller. What is it with us southern English folk, eh? Bunch of uptight, miserable arseholes, aren't we?

'I'm sorry we don't have many friends, darling,' I said.

'It's not your fault at all.'

'No, but you had lots of friends before you met me, so I kind of feel like it's because of me that you don't have any now.'

'Not at all, babe. It's just more difficult to make friends down here because you English folk are a bunch of uptight, miserable arseholes,' she said. My thought exactly.

'But you love us.' I leaned over and kissed her on the cheek.

'You're alright…' she said as she dipped a piece of fake chicken deep into the tub of sour cream to mask the cardboard taste.

I've been working from home for the past five years, and yes, working from home means that I'm able to do my washing, clean my shower and play Candy Crush all while hosting a meeting, but it also means that I am, without being too dramatic, devastatingly lonely.

My English teacher in secondary school once told me that loneliness is a killer, which had nothing to do with the dull-arse book we were reading, but that phrase has stuck with me ever since.

Loneliness *is* a killer. And boy, am I lonely. I want to

63

have friends, someone to tell my awful jokes to (Cat has heard all of them thousands of times), someone I can show off to, invite to the beach on the busiest day of the year and practise being myself with. I can be myself 100 per cent in front of Cat. I'm sure if I shat in my hands and clapped she'd just chuckle and ask me what's for dinner. (Make it yourself, darling, I've just shat in my hands.)

But how the hell do you make friends as an adult? I've always been terrible at making friends; it's just something that has never come naturally to me. Also, I don't ever want kids so it's not like I'm going to make some friends in my womb and then give birth to them. I'm not saying that's the *only* reason why people have kids, but having someone to go to the cinema with and who will one day organise your funeral has certainly got to be a factor when deciding whether to procreate or not.

So, if I'm never going to have children, I think I need to do something about the whole lack-of-friends thing. Before the crippling loneliness *really* takes hold.

> **Earl:** Are you saying that you could feel *even* lonelier?
> **Me:** Yes.
> **Earl:** Fantastic! I was starting to worry that you'd peaked already.

My first memory of feeling lonely was when I was seven years old. Picture the scene: a young, awkward Jenna with her buck teeth, wonky fringe and ugly school shoes standing in the playground next to her very best friend Emily. Emily and I got on like a house on fire doused in petrol located in the pits of hell, and in my mind we were going to be best friends forever, and only death would part us.

However, one lunchtime on a rainy Tuesday (but to be honest I can't really remember the *exact* day, it could've been a sunny Wednesday), the worst thing happened… Emily was invited to join the popular kids in the

SCREWED UP, SLIMMED DOWN

playground, and I wasn't.

After not being able to find my invitation to join the popular kids, I started locking myself in the toilet cubicle at lunchtime. The feeling of hurt and rejection swam through my chubby little body as I scoffed my tearstained biscuits and wondered why I'd been left out.

After a couple of weeks of this, the dinner ladies eventually coaxed me out of the locked toilets and I was forced to either stand in the middle of the playground on my own like a stupid goose or gang up.

Reader, I chose to gang up. I ganged up with the only people who would have me: the weird kids. It was me and my fellow oddballs from then on, and anything, I mean *anything* could've parted us: a rainy day, a windy day or even the slight promise of joining another group that was even just a *tiny* bit cooler than we were.

When I was growing up, every school playground had a group of weird kids. You knew that they were the weird kids just by looking at them. We were all different, not in a negative way, just in a way that screamed 'WE DON'T FIT IN, PLEASE BULLY US'. There was me – I was the fat kid who was definitely going to be a lesbian – a girl called Erin, who was so shy she avoided mirrors, and smelly Lucy, whose family went LARPing at the weekends.

There I was, for the first (and not the last) time in my life making friends with people who, although lovely and only slightly strange, weren't my tribe. *My* tribe is fun, goofy and dark-humoured, but young Jenna soon learnt that she wasn't good enough to be friends with those sorts of people. So since then I've just become friends with anyone who will have me, regardless of whether a) I like them, b) we have anything in common, or c) I actually enjoy being in their company.

I've still not found my tribe. I imagine one day I'll drive past a roundabout and in the middle of it will be my tribe waving big placards that read, 'Hey, Jenna, we're your tribe!' But even if I *did* find my tribe, I don't think I'll ever be able to approach them because a) they'd be stranded in the middle of a roundabout, and b) fundamentally, I believe that everyone else is superior to me and I'm not worthy of being around anyone. They'll soon think that I'm just a desperate, fat bore who irritates and annoys everyone.

Earl: You forgot to mention that you're also a negative Nancy who sees the worst in every situation.
Me: Oh yeah, thanks, I get that from you.
Earl: I'm so giving.

My true self is goofy, loud and silly. But if you've ever had the privilege (or unfortunate luck depending on how you feel about me) of being in my company then you'll know that I am not those things in public. Around my guinea pigs and Cat, yes, I'm the life of the living room. But in front of others? Absolutely not. They might judge me and make me feel like a weird twatting idiot. Must shrink down and hide back into my people-pleasing shell!

BUT THIS IS ABOUT TO CHANGE. I will no longer settle for anyone who will 'just have me'! I *am* worth being friends with, I am not *that* boring and nor am I *that* irritating. When I first started this transformation year I knew that being able to be 100 per cent myself was going to be one of the biggest challenges that I'd have to tackle.

Wanda: Let's tackle this bitch!!
Me: Calm it, Wanda.
Wanda: TACKLE IT TO DEEEEEATH!!!!

My new 'I will be 100 per cent myself' campaign was put to the test last night when a new friend from tennis, Sarah, invited a few of us out for her birthday drinks. Now, I hadn't socialised with these people beyond tennis before, so I was a tad (read: horrendously) nervous.

I feel like I can be myself a lot more at tennis because I

SCREWED UP, SLIMMED DOWN

haven't got time to keep my people-pleasing mask in place. Sure, I still try to rein it in a bit by not celebrating too hard and not smashing my racket against my face when I miss a shot (please, I never miss a shot). But everyone else is so distracted with their own tennis that they're not paying attention to what I'm doing, so I'm free to be myself. HOWEVER, now that we were just going to be sat drinking in a bar, they were *actually* going to see what I was really like. Shit…

> **Earl:** These people are going to realise you're a knob within three minutes.
> **Wanda:** You're going to have a great time, Jenna. Just be yourself!
> **Earl:** Jesus, don't be yourself or they'll realise you're a knob before you've even walked through the door.
> **Wanda:** Let your true personality come out, Jenna. You have so much to offer.
> **Earl:** Yeah, like a lift home…
> **Wanda:** You got this, girl, go and have fun. If you don't enjoy it, don't do it again. Simple.

Cat dropped me off at Haywards Heath train station and I quickly ran into the shop to grab a can of lager before getting the train down to Brighton. Yes, I know it's not good to manage anxiety with alcohol but I felt so nervous that the manic bunnies in my stomach were jumping around more than usual.

The evening was lovely. God, it was so good. Being yourself really makes life more fun, doesn't it? Well, unless the people you're being yourself around don't appreciate your true self, but if that's the case then sod them, they're clearly not your people.

There was only one moment when I spoke absolute twaddle and didn't make a word of sense, and that was to a guy called Steve. Steve had said something that I didn't totally hear/understand/listen to, so when I replied all that

SCREWED UP, SLIMMED DOWN

came out was a load of nonsense.

'I've got to take my mum out tomorrow, it's good to take her out, she'll like that. But I've got to bring my son with me, so that'll be interesting,' he said. Did he say that? I'm not totally sure, because like I said before, I couldn't hear him, what with the bar being noisy and me not actually listening.

'Well, I guess that's good, until it isn't. Hopefully, it'll be quick,' I replied.

He paused for a moment.

'Sorry, I didn't really understand what you just said,' he said, leaning in closer in case the reason why he didn't understand me was because he couldn't hear me.

'Yeah, I'm not totally sure I understand what I just said either,' I laughed, which made him laugh too. And that worked. I spoke absolute bollocks, something that the real me does quite a bit because I've got problems with speech, comprehension and making any bloody sense. But all I had to do was acknowledge the fact that I spoke absolute bollocks and it was fine.

No more pretending like I know what I'm talking about. I haven't got a clue what I'm going on about half the time and I'm proud of it (well, I'm not proud of it, but it's a thing I do). And sometimes the things that come out of my mouth are funny and making people laugh is my only goal in life.

Besides becoming disgustingly rich and famous obviously.

CHAPTER 12

I'M DULLER THAN A CLIPBOARD

'So you're not happy in your relationship and you think that ending it would be the best thing for both of you, but you're scared?' my new therapist asked me today, like it was the stupidest thing he'd ever heard.

I've decided to go to therapy again after having stopped doing it a few years ago during the pandemic because the face-to-face sessions had to move online, and I only do online meetings if I'm contractually obliged to do them.

My new therapist is a very posh-looking straight man who wears clothes from Cotton Traders, sits cross-legged and avoids all eye contact, choosing instead to stare at his clipboard.

My first thought was, 'Ooh, he has a clipboard, he must be very serious about my therapy because my last therapist just had a tiny notebook that he hardly ever wrote in,' but it turns out that the clipboard is just a distraction for his eyes because, like teenage Jenna, he hates eye contact.

'Yes…' I mumbled, crossing my arms tightly to my chest. 'I think that if we break up, I'll never find love again.'

'Do you *really* believe that?' he asked in disbelief.

'Absolutely. I believe that if Cat and I break up then I'll immediately regret it and then it'll be too late to go back, or if we *did* break up and it turned out to actually be for the best, I won't ever find anyone who will love me like Cat does,' I told him.

I've been to a few different therapists throughout my life and although my experience at the hypnotherapy sessions earlier in the year went well, there wasn't really enough time during the sessions for me to talk about everything that's on my mind (bitch needs a lot of time for that).

Psychotherapy gives me a chance to talk endlessly about my problems without worrying if I'm boring the pants off the therapist, because they're being paid to sit and listen. Also, recently I've realised that I like to create a codependent relationship with my therapists, which is probably the most healthy form of codependency there is. Do you think that's why therapists are so bloody understanding and nice? So that you'll be codependent on them and never leave?

Although, I did once have a therapist who ghosted me. I emailed asking to book in another session with her and she totally ignored me. I guess it *is* possible to bore the pants off a therapist.

'So, aside from your relationship, how is the rest of your life?' he asked, scribbling on his clipboard.

'Well, I'm going through a bit of a transformation year at the moment, where I'm working on my physical and mental health, so I've been trying to get out of my comfort zone, which is terribly inconvenient, because my comfort zone is *really* bloody comfortable.'

He chuckled a tiny chuckle. Oh no, dude, if you want to carry on being my therapist you're going to have to laugh a lot harder at my jokes.

'And how are you trying to get out of your comfort zone?'

'Well, yesterday I went wild swimming in the sea and it

was 10 degrees Celsius. "Uncomfortable" doesn't even *begin* to cover it,' I told him.

This crazy idea came to me last week when I was chomping down on my dinner while watching a Netflix documentary where a crazy Dutch guy called Wim Hoff told minge-candle-maker Gwyneth Paltrow about cold-water therapy.

According to the documentary, cold-water therapy is really good for both your mind and body as it boosts the immune system, is good for your cardiovascular system AND it can improve symptoms of depression and anxiety.

Well, that sounded like a bit of what I'm bloody well after…

'That would be a good way for me to get out of my comfort zone,' I said to Cat, before remembering the fact that cold-water therapy means that I would actually have get into cold water.

'Cool, let's go to the beach tomorrow,' she suggested.

'What, noooooo, I need to build up to it. I can't just dive in at the deep end. Pun intended.' I got out my phone and started to Google more about it. 'The internet tells me I need to start by having cold showers.'

'Sounds awful, darling.'

So, the next day I popped my gorgeous flabby body into the shower, washed my body and my bits and then stood there staring at the temperature nozzle. It was on red (Level: Scorch) – could I turn it down?

Wanda: Yes, Jenna! Turn it down!

I turned the nozzle down slightly.

Me: Oh, that's a wee bit chilly.

My body adjusted to the slight drop in warmth. I turned the nozzle down further.

SCREWED UP, SLIMMED DOWN

Me: Oooh, OK, that's very chilly.

I turned the nozzle the entire way, down to the coldest blue (Level: Arctic).

Me: Holy Christ, that's fecking freezing.

The water was shocking. My skin stung with the cold as I tried to focus on calming my breath. My mind was empty; I was no longer partaking in the arguments that I normally have with myself in the shower because the only thing I could think of was to breathe. Just breathe. I turned like a kebab woman in the shower, letting the freezing water get to every bit of my body. Surprisingly, I managed to stay under the cold shower for a good 20 seconds before jumping out shrieking and grabbing the towel to manically rub myself down.

The stinging eventually stopped and suddenly, something amazing happened – my mind was clear.

I felt alive and it felt bloody brilliant. So brilliant, in fact, that I've been having a cold ending to my shower every day for a week. But yesterday, it was time to level up.

Before setting off to Worthing beach in the morning, I Googled the temperature of the water and, apparently, it's colder than my ex-girlfriend's heart. That's a lie – a) I don't have an ex-girlfriend, and b) even if I did, by the time I'd finished with her she wouldn't have a heart left in her body (that's right, if you break my heart then I'm going to eat yours).

Earl: Too weird, Jenna, calm down.

Cat came with me to the beach but refused to get into the water. She just stood on the shore waiting for me with a towel, a hot-water bottle and a flask of tea.

As I stepped into the sea, my feet disappeared into the numbing water and I began to wonder whether this was what cryopreservation feels like, not that anyone alive would ever know. I guess when those people who have died and been cryopreserved come back to life we can ask them.

Anyhoo, never one to dilly-dally, I quickly marched into the water. My ankles, fecking freezing, my legs, fecking freezing, my fanny, oh my God, I've never felt cold like it. Moving in deeper, the shocking water rose from my fanny to my belly, then to my chest (breathe, Jenna, breathe) and finally my shoulders.

'What's it like?' Cat shouted.

'My nipples have frozen off!' I shrieked, manically swimming about trying to warm myself up.

I swam and swam, my legs kicking and my arms flapping about under the water like I was doing the Gangnam Style dance at double speed. I didn't even have any wee in me to warm myself up. But after a minute of splashing about the warmth finally came. (I use the term 'warmth' very loosely here.)

While I was in the Baltic ocean, my mind was calm again, there were no anxieties, no overthinking, no 'what is the point in life, death and all that nonsense'. It was just clear, and I was present.

I think that's what makes cold-water therapy so great for the old noggin; it takes you away from those arguments in your head (which I *never* win, which makes zero sense because I normally play both parts of the argument) and it brings you into the present moment: the cold, the shock, your breath, right here, right now.

'So, would you do it again?' Cat asked on the drive home.

'Christ, no,' I said, shivering in the passenger seat and hugging the hot-water bottle tightly. 'It was fun, though, but no, next time I go wild swimming it'll be in a place like Barbados during the height of summer after a few piña coladas.'

I've gotten used to doing the cold water bit at the end

of my shower, so going forward I will keep doing that as it helps set me up for the day. But at the request of my vagina (who never wants to be that cold again), it's a big fat no to cold-water swimming.

CHAPTER 13

THE FAT JUST MELTS OFF

I've been doing 'Jenna's form of keto' for a good three months now and to begin with it was going smashingly. Apparently, it really *was* my exclusively brown and beige diet that had been keeping me fat and *not* my antidepressants at all... God, I'd better not tell my mother. I'd hate to prove her right, again.

Things in my relationship still aren't going well. A few weeks ago we made a list of what we both need to do in order to improve things, and that lasted a few days, but we've both slowly slipped back into old habits. Me avoiding talking about my feelings, her staying up till 3 am playing her PlayStation. Me thinking that there must be more to life than this and her not bothering to do anything with her life besides work in a job she hates. I love her, but she doesn't really *do* anything, and I don't (or rather, didn't before this fancy transformational year started) do much either. We're both just pouring from an empty cup.

Throwing myself into this weight loss and fitness thing

instead of focusing on my troubled relationship is helping me keep just the tiniest bit sane. It's the only thing I'm able to control at the moment and since the beginning of the year I've lost a stone, which is *fantastic* and not at all a slow dribble, what with it being April already.

One stone in four months doesn't sound great; however, when I was my biggest (four years ago at 19 stone) it was easier to lose weight quicker because I had so much more blubber to lose. But now that I'm just obese and not morbidly obese, frustratingly, it's coming off a tad slower.

My goal to fit into a size 'Medium' is... well, quite frankly, still far away at this point (even though I now fit into an XL), because in the last two weeks I haven't actually lost anything and I feel like my weight loss has plateaued. Hmm, 'Jenna's form of keto' clearly isn't enough for me to drop three to four stone and become super-fit and sexy. I need a *new* plan.

The other week when I was at Sarah's birthday drinks something amazing happened when I moved seats and sat next to Julian, another new friend from tennis.

'You've lost weight, haven't you?' Julian said as I sat down next to him.

'Why, yes, I have, thank you so much for noticing,' I replied, plumping the bottom of my hair for extra comic effect.

'I lost a lot of weight too – look, here's me five stone heavier,' he said, showing me a picture of his bigger frame on his phone. I grabbed the phone and then looked up at the guy in front of me, a slip of a man who you wouldn't have thought had *any* issues with weight.

I grabbed his arm.

'Tell. Me. How.'

He told me that it was something called intermittent fasting. I'd sort of heard of the phrase before, but I thought it was just some rubbish trend that influencers got paid to talk about. I was wrong.

'I just eat between the hours of 12 pm and 8 pm. I haven't had breakfast for three years,' he said. Initially, I thought that sounded like a load of twaddle, because I've been brought up being told that breakfast is the most important meal of the day and if you don't eat little and often then you'll be the size of a house forever.

'It's not good to keep eating, actually. Your body works better when it's not constantly releasing insulin. Honestly, the fat just melts off,' he added.

'I JUST WANT MY FAT TO MELT OFF!' I said with all seriousness, putting my beer down. If I could give birth to my fat I *would*, but if there's something that could cause it to just 'melt' off, then bloody brilliant!

In my drunken buzz on the train ride home, I Googled the shit out of intermittent fasting with the phrase 'the fat just melts off' still ringing in my ears.

Basically, it turns out that we're all doing the whole eating thing wrong and we should all immediately start intermittent fasting.

Earl: What the hell is intermittent fasting?
Me: It's where you only eat within an eight-hour window and then fast for 16 hours, which sounds like a long time but, if you're like me, 12 of those hours are spent sleeping so… it's easier than you think.
Wanda: Apparently there are so many health benefits to intermittent fasting; I think it sounds great!
Earl: So you can't eat or drink anything for 16 hours?
Me: I can drink water, tea and coffee. But no sugar, milk or 'food' liquids.
Earl: Milk isn't food.
Me: Try telling that to a baby.

So, with all the research complete, I decided that the next day would be the first day of intermittent fasting, even with my hangover. The new chapter in my weight-loss journey had begun.

SCREWED UP, SLIMMED DOWN

I'm not going to lie, the first day was a bitch. I had all the acid reflux and nausea, because my body is so used to being fed within 30 seconds of waking from its slumber that my stomach had already prepared the volcano of acid which it normally needs to digest my massive breakfast.

But no more, nuh-uh… That acid can sit and bubble away at my stomach lining because I am *now* an intermittent faster. On the first morning I filled up with so much orange squash and green tea that I spent most of the morning rushing to the toilet. I guess the money I'll save from skipping breakfast will have to go towards my increased toilet roll bill.

As 12 o'clock crept slowly closer I continued to drink and wee tea. So much tea, so much wee. When the window of eating finally arrived I was ready with my knife and fork staring manically between the clock and my two fried eggs, mushrooms, tomatoes and spinach on a bed of thin brown bread.

As I took that first bite I instantly came in my pants. OK, that's a bit of an exaggeration, but it did taste amazing. So, hunger makes food taste better. Interesting…

For the rest of that first day I ate normally – one snack, a protein shake and dinner. I always finish my dinner well before 8 pm so that wasn't going to be a problem.

The only problem I could foresee was the evening snacking. You know, when one is watching a movie or a TV show, or reading a book, or literally doing anything, one needs a snack. Well, it seemed that I was going to have to fit all my snacks in before 8 pm.

Previously, I've tried brushing my teeth earlier in the evening to discourage me from all the snacking, but I would just cave and then have to endure Colgate-flavoured chocolate rather than the pure stuff.

In the first week I dropped four pounds (and no, that wasn't just from a big poo). Since then I've been steadily losing weight, and actually, the whole not eating before 12 pm and after 8 pm is surprisingly bloody easy. I think

SCREWED UP, SLIMMED DOWN

I'll intermittently fast permanently from now on. It's a lifestyle, bbz, not a diet. Yes, I know I sound like a pretentious knob.

Earl: You said it.

CHAPTER 14

MY FANNY HAS DIED

May

I don't want to be too inappropriate, but sometimes I think my fanny has died. (It wasn't the cold-water swimming that killed it off, by the way, me having a dead vagina is a pre-existing condition.) The disappearance of my genitals could be because of my antidepressants *or* my current awful mental health. Or both… But whatever the cause, it's an issue, especially in a doughnut-bumper relationship, because the thing that distinguishes two female friends and two lesbian lovers is the 'lovers' bit.

According to the Google, being fat also decreases sex drive, though I'm sure there are lots of people out there who will say that they are obese and shagging every day. Well, good for you. Though if I really think about it, I was having more sex when I was bigger, so that blows that theory out of the water.

What if I've just become one of those people who doesn't have any sexy feelings? Am I asexual? (Machine!) No, I'm definitely not asexual. There have been times in the past when I've had all the sexy feelings in my pants, it's just that right now my vagina has decided to take a

SCREWED UP, SLIMMED DOWN

sabbatical. Right when my relationship needs it to very much be present! Bad fanny!

Is it lesbian bed death? Is it the relationship? Or is it me? I have a feeling it's me. Shit... This isn't fair on Cat.

So not only am I putting her through all the crap with my mental health, doubts, anxieties and panic attacks, but I'm also not able to give her what she needs physically.

Wanda: Maybe it's time to give both of you a break and separate.

Me: What?! But I can't do life without her. It'll destroy me.

Wanda: But you can't both keep living like this. You've both gone a bit... stale. And there's a life to live out there, Jenna. For both of you!

Earl: Stale is safe. Life is dangerous. Stay at home.

Me: What, stuck in despair with a dead fanny? I feel like I've lost myself.

Wanda: Sometimes you need to break something to fix it. Sometimes you need to lose someone to find yourself.

Earl: God, that's wanky.

Wanda: What would you say to your friend if they were in the same situation?

Earl: How about 'Stop wasting my time with all your moaning?'

Me: I'd tell them that sometimes the kindest thing is to let go, and if it's meant to be, then you will come back to each other.

Wanda: There you go.

Me: Oh, bollocks...

CHAPTER 15

MY GUINEA PIG IS IN THE BLOODY WAY

I don't particularly like my therapist. He's constantly glued to his clipboard – and unless he's planning on writing a book about me being the most interesting and messed-up case he's ever dealt with (doubtful, unfortunately), then eyes up and pen down, mate! Also, he has the personality of a spoon. Not that I want him to be cracking all the jokes or anything (though it would be nice if he laughed at a few more of mine), but seriously, I feel like I'm the one trying to lighten the mood. And also, it's me who's meant to be avoiding eye contact and acting all weird and insecure, not him.

So today I had my penultimate session before I move on to a new therapist. Preferably one without a clipboard.

'Have you ever heard of Carl Jung?' he asked me earlier.

'Will Young?'

'No, Carl Jung. He was a psychoanalyst and he had a lot of theories on people's dreams and the unconscious mind. I'd like to try one of his experiments with you. You

SCREWED UP, SLIMMED DOWN

just need to close your eyes and think of the first thing that comes into your mind when I give you the prompts. Don't tell me what the things are right away, I'll ask at the end and then we can go through what they mean. Does that sound OK?'

'Absolutely.'

'OK, good. Now, close your eyes and imagine you're in a forest walking down a path. What type of path is it? What's it made of? Is it night or day? Is it warm or is it chilly? Now, you're walking down the path when you see an obstacle in your way – what is that obstacle? You then come across a cup on the floor, you bend down and pick it up. What is it made of? Is there any liquid inside? You then see a key on the floor and you pick it up. What type of key is it? What does it unlock? What do you do with the key? You then reach the end of the path where there's a large wall – what's on the other side of the wall? OK, you can open your eyes now.'

I opened my eyes. 'Right, let's start at the beginning,' he said, clicking his pen and scribbling something on his clipboard. Probably drawing a cock and balls or something. No, that would be *far* too humorous for him.

'What was the path made of?' he asked.

'Broken glass,' I replied.

'Broken glass? Hmmm.' He thought for a moment. 'That represents pain. So whichever direction you choose is going to be painful.' Well, duh. But also, yeah, that's actually stupidly accurate. If I stay with Cat it will cause pain; if I leave, it will cause pain. Which is the better pain?

'And tell me about the forest.'

'The forest was cold, dark and scary.'

'OK, so that's pretty self-explanatory. And what was the obstacle?'

'The obstacle was Rusty, one of my guinea pigs. He was stood in the middle of the path and I couldn't get by him.' Which makes *no* sense because in real life he's just a fluffy little potato.

SCREWED UP, SLIMMED DOWN

'It would seem that the obstacle that's stopping you from moving forward at the moment is your home life.'

'Yeah, that makes sense,' I said, as a wave of sadness suddenly hit me.

'And what about the cup?' he asked.

'The cup was empty and I ate it because it was made of chocolate,' I said, which made him look up from his clipboard.

'You ate it?' He laughed.

Finally! A laugh… God is good.

'Yes, I took a big bite out of it, and although it looked like a regular porcelain cup it was actually made out of chocolate.'

'Hmm, interesting. And what about the key?'

'That was a Haribo key that didn't unlock anything. I ate that too.'

'Hmm, what I'm getting from your answers about the cup and the key is that you're playful, but it could also mean that there's some childhood trauma there that needs to be dealt with. And lastly, what was on the other side of the wall?'

'On the other side of the wall was a large grassy park. It was summer and there were loads of people in small groups having picnics, throwing frisbees and just having fun.'

'I see… So it's quite obvious what all of your answers represent, but it's good to do these sorts of experiments to really understand what is going on within your subconscious.'

Yeah, so basically I'm in a dark, depressing place where any move will cause me pain and it's my home life and unhealed childhood trauma that's stopping me from moving forward. Well, that was £45 well spent.

CHAPTER 16

THERE'LL BE NO SEX IN THIS HOT TUB

Last weekend Cat and I almost broke up. We went to stay in a romantic lodge in Norfolk – it was her treat which made me feel even worse. Oh, look, your girlfriend is so kind and lovely and you're just a big horrible monster who's ruining the relationship.

The weekend was an opportunity for us to relax and hopefully get back to being us away from home. Away from the prison that is our flat and to, hopefully, gain some clarity on the doubts and anxieties that plague my mind.

On the Friday night, we went out for a meal and then had a walk in the forest, where we held hands and saw a baby deer. It was lovely and for a brief hour it was how things used to be.

On the Saturday, I spent most of the day sitting in the hot tub on the veranda of our beautiful lodge overlooking the countryside and watching the Madrid Open tennis tournament on my iPad. What's better than that? Not bloody much! Well, apart from the fact that Cat was inside

SCREWED UP, SLIMMED DOWN

watching TV and all the doubts were still messing with my mind.

As I sat there going wrinkly like a prune, I knew deep down that Cat and I have just become best friends – we're spending our romantic weekend away in separate rooms. But we're so extremely codependent that breaking up feels like cold-blooded murder.

In the evening we were both in the hot tub looking up at the night sky, just like we had done in our private pool in Bali. On that special night in Bali the song 'Wishing on a Star' was playing on my phone and we danced and kissed and looked up at the stars while we melted in our pool of love (I know, puke). But now, back in the hot tub in Norfolk, the clouds were slowly creeping across the sky and we were not in a pool of love.

'You doing OK?' Cat asked me, knowing full well that I wasn't. Seriously, this woman can read me like a book. I can drop just a tiny bit mood-wise and her spidey-senses will pick it up and jump on it straight away.

'Yeah, I'm fine,' I lied.

'Jenna Wimshurst, I know you.'

'Sorry… It's just we're here in this lovely setting and I just can't get rid of this black cloud of doom.'

'What's it focusing on?' she asked.

I paused, struggling to find the words.

'Is it me?'

'Yeah…' I looked down at the water, unable to meet her eyes.

'OK… What's it saying?'

'That we're just best friends,' I said, still not looking at her. 'I love you so much, so, so much, but my gut is saying that we're not making each other happy and I've been having this anxiety for a while now and… it just doesn't feel right.'

We continued to speak some more and Cat told me that she too had been thinking that the relationship wasn't right, but she didn't want it to end either.

SCREWED UP, SLIMMED DOWN

'I love you,' I said, swimming over to her side of the hot tub to hug her tightly. Suddenly the tears came hard and fast.

'I love you too.' Cat squeezed me hard. 'But I don't know how much longer I can do this, babe.' Oh shit… there's her breaking point. 'I love you, but I'm not happy.'

I pulled out of the hug and wiped away my tears, but it was useless because they just kept coming.

'Me too.'

'So, what do we do?' she asked.

'I don't know.'

'Do you want to break up?'

'No! No. But… I don't see any other way out of this unhappiness that we're both in,' I said through more tears. How the hell can I break something that's so special to me? It's the only thing that's been keeping me going. But it's wrong. It's wrong and we both know it. 'I'm struggling, I can't do this Cat, I can't do this.'

'Well, I'm not going to break us up, so if you want to break up then you have to do it.'

'No, I mean I can't do this, I'm having a panic attack.' The panic hit me like a fucking train. Hard. Fast. Zero warning. 'I need to go in, I feel like I'm having a nervous breakdown.'

'It's OK, babe. Everything is going to be OK.' She rubbed my leg as I stepped out of the hot tub. 'I'll be in in a minute, I'm just going to have a cigarette,' she added, clearly needing to process what had just happened. Or, *nearly* happened.

I rushed into the bedroom, swallowed a propranolol and sobbed naked on the bed in what was one of the lowest points of my life. (Which is ironic, because I *thought* that I was at rock bottom during that panic attack in Edinburgh. But it turns out that my rock bottom actually has a secret wine cellar. Just with no bloody wine in it.)

Cat told me that she wasn't sure how long she could take me having doubts. She said that it's crushing her self-confidence. Of course it is. Of *course* it is. God, I need to fix this mess.

The next day Cat and I went to a drive-through safari park and it was nice and fun and normal, though I was mentally drained. I spent the car ride back down to Haywards Heath Googling 'How to prevent a mental breakdown'. I feel like I'm so close to really losing it mentally. I feel like I'm so close to having a proper psychotic episode.

Something nearly flipped in my mind in that hot tub. I felt like I was just moments away from losing all control over my mental faculties.

I always thought that I was nuts, but in a fun way, not in a 'Shit, we need to section Jenna' kind of way.

CHAPTER 17

WOW, THIS SUCKS…

Cat and I are no more. At 11 am today, I walked out of my kitchen and into my second bedroom where Cat, the love of my life and partner of eight years, was sitting working at her desk. I leaned against the wall beside her and slid down it slowly, tears running down my face. She swivelled in her chair to face me. She knew.

'My darling, I love you more than anything in the world, but I can't do this anymore,' I said, staring at the floor through flooded eyes. 'We're stuck in a rut and I can't see any way out of it for us. We've tried and tried, but it's not working. I want you to be happy and I'm not making you happy. I'm not happy, so how can I make you happy?'

Cat stared down at me and was silent for a moment. 'Are we breaking up?' she mumbled. A fresh rush of hot tears fell from my eyes and a stab of pain punched me in my stomach.

'I think it's the only thing left for us to do,' I said, watching as her eyes started to fill with tears. She nodded and looked down at her feet. 'I love you,' I continued, 'I will always love you. I'm so sorry, love. I'm so, so sorry.'

I closed my eyes and let the hot tears fall, the pain crushing me.

'I love you too. But I think you're right,' was all she could muster in response.

We sat in silence for a few minutes, both staring at our feet. Neither of us had wanted this to happen, but sometimes the Universe is a dick and breaking something is the only way to make it better. In the long run, at least, not the short run – in the short run breakups fucking suck.

Cat swivelled her office chair back to face her desk and closed her laptop slowly. 'I'm going to go to Jamie's house for the rest of the day,' she said, standing up, still staring at her feet.

I put my hand out for her to help me up off the floor. She yanked me up and I pulled her tightly into my arms, weeping hard into her shoulder. I never wanted to let her go.

Have I done the right thing? Have I done the worst thing? Only time will tell… All I know is that at the moment I'm full of sadness, tears and heartbreak. I love her so much and I never want to be without her and life will suck so bad without her. But I need to give myself (and her) a chance to be happy again. I'm doing this for her. For us.

I know that one day we will look back and know that it was the right thing for us. I need to sort myself out, on my own. I will be happy again. She will be happy again. And this *will* be the right thing to have done. But for now, it sucks hard and I'm going to binge eat while I cry my soul out on my bed.

……

It's been a week since we broke up and I haven't stopped crying. I'm going to miss her so much. She's my person. I'm going to be Thelma without Louise, which is exactly

SCREWED UP, SLIMMED DOWN

the problem – Thelma and Louise were best friends, not lovers.

Life is going to suck without Cat but we have both lost ourselves and we need to heal if we ever have the chance of being happy together again.

It's going to hurt like a bitch and the pain will overwhelm me, but it will get easier. I hope.

… Eight years we've been together. That's eight years of morphing into each other. Buying the same clothes, finishing each other's sentences, knowing what the other is thinking and feeling without even being in the same room as each other.

CHAPTER 18

MY CUP OF SELF-CARE IS BLOODY EMPTY

June

Apparently, self-care means more than just a wank in a fancy bubble bath. If there's ever a time when I need to give myself some self-care, it's right now; as I go through my first breakup. As breakups go I've given myself a real humdinger to start with… Eight years we've been together. That's eight years of morphing into each other. Buying the same clothes, finishing each other's sentences, knowing what the other is thinking and feeling without even being in the same room as each other.

I've forgotten who I am without Cat and I'm terrified to find out. What if I'm a total arsehole? Christ, I hope I'm not an arsehole.

Earl: The chances are high though, aren't they?

The day after Cat and I broke up we exchanged on the sale of our flat (is this the Universe telling me that it was the right decision to separate? Hmmm…).

SCREWED UP, SLIMMED DOWN

It's been two weeks since Cat and I split up and, as you can imagine, it's been hell. We've both cried every day, though it's mainly me who's in a constant flood of tears. I would walk into a room, or we'd be sitting next to each other having dinner and I'd just start bursting into tears at the fact that, in a few weeks' time, I won't be living with my person anymore. I've been so close, *so* many times to changing my mind. But I know, deep, deep down, that it's the best thing for both of us.

Since we've broken up, nothing physically has changed. We still sleep in the same bed, we still have dinner together, kiss each other goodnight and tell each other we love each other, just like before. Basically, *nothing* has changed, but we've only got one month left until we complete on the sale of the flat so our days together are numbered.

We have one month to, a) find somewhere else to live (separately) and, b) live with each other as best as we can while also navigating this horrendous heartbreak. Cat is planning on moving to Kent to be near some of her family and I'm moving down near Hove to be near my tennis club.

Flat-wise, I'm looking for anything that isn't a box room where I have to eat, sleep and shit all in the same room. I will NOT go through my breakup while slumming it, thank you very much. I need at least two bedrooms, an en-suite and to be within a 15-minute drive of the tennis club, which I imagine I will be frequenting a lot more to stop myself from crying into oblivion. If there's one thing that's going to help me through this, it's a shitload of tennis. And a shitload of self-help.

Enter, stage right: every self-help book I've ever bought and not read. According to the first one I picked up, self-care includes saying 'no' to things you don't want to do and saying 'yes' to things you do want to do.

'Do I want to pay this electricity bill?' No.

'Do I want another pint?' Yes.

SCREWED UP, SLIMMED DOWN

OK, so perhaps not quite like that. Let's separate my life into three sections to see how I should self-care the hell out of them.

Physical: Obviously, this year is all about my physical health, so I will continue to eat what is good for my body. Multipacks of Wagon Wheels are *not* good for my health, no matter how much I try to convince myself that there's real strawberries in the jam.

Social: Am I getting enough social interaction? Well, in a month's time I'm going to be alone, so in order to not return to the isolated lonely hermit crab that I was before I met Cat, I need to continue to meet other fellow human beings. This will include but not be limited to: meeting up with people from tennis, getting in touch with old friends who I've neglected and texting at least one person a day. Seriously, I can go for days without talking to anyone other than Cat. God, what am I doing? Breaking from the one person in the world who gets me?

> **Wanda:** Jenna, focus! There are loads of people out there who will get you.

Mental: Right, onto the next bit: mental shizz. I must continue meditating, even though, let's be real here, it's a drag. Also, I must refrain from getting plastered when I'm out doing the aforementioned social interaction stuff. I'm sure I can enjoy a night out and still stick to just the three beers, I don't have to have six and then have the beer fear the next day. Also, I must block Adele from my Spotify, read only happy news stories and consume only funny things on the TV.

I'm a delicate little poppet who feels everything, so if I hear a ballad, read a sad story or watch a show with even a *hint* of sadness then it will open up Jenna's box of undealt-with trauma and WE DON'T WANT THAT, DO WE?

SCREWED UP, SLIMMED DOWN

Earl: Christ, no.

When people say 'self-care' I always think of candles, a luxury massage or buying myself some expensive fluffy slippers that I won't wear, because who under the age of 85 wears slippers?

But no, self-care means putting *yourself* first. This is something that I've always struggled with because I'm a people-pleaser so I like putting other people's needs before my own in the hope that they'll love me.

Wanda: What about adding boundaries?
Me: Who?
Wanda: Self-kindness?
Me: Never heard of her.
Wanda: Self-validation?
Me: It's like you're speaking French.
Wanda: I'm saying that you need to be kind to yourself, put your needs first and find validation from within.
Earl: That's the funniest thing I've ever heard.
Me: Right?!

Now, back to the breakup thing. I have a few questions… By the way, I'm going to use humour to deflect from the horror of my breakup for as long as possible, so please bear with me.

What do you do with your sex toys after a breakup? Neither of us can use them again, obviously, not only because we've both promised to never love again, but also because if for some crazy reason we *did* ever get it on with someone else, well, no one wants a second-hand dildo, do they? Although, if you think about it, a penis is essentially 'second-hand' and I'd trust my OCD-like cleaning rituals over any man's. No offence, men, but I've heard about your poor attempts at willy cleaning – sort it out, lads.

I've never been through a proper split before, so I'm new to the practicalities (not to mention the emotional grief) of a breakup. The last time I had my heart crushed was when I was 18, but that was just some unrequited love with my school best friend. So although that heartache was intense, it's nothing like my current breakup, because Cat and I have made an entire life together. My school best friend and I had barely made a daisy chain.

Apart from finally understanding what it is that Adele is actually singing about (though she is banned from my playlists, I tell you, BANNED), what the hell do you do in a breakup?

Do we do the lesbian thing and stay best friends? When should I leave her family WhatsApp group? And who gets to keep the drill?

Over the past two weeks, with our bravest faces on, we've gone through each room in our flat and separated every single thing we own. And it's been fine, until we started to separate the important stuff, things like the TV – who gets that? Well, if she gets the TV then I get the Dyson… And who gets to keep the yucca plant that we've both spent years carefully tending to with special organic plant food?

And what about getting dressed and having a shower? Do we both have to do that in private now? We're still making each other dinner and doing our washing together, but suddenly boobies and bums are non-shareable. Weird.

When it came to the guinea pigs, we were at a stalemate. I'm more attentive to them, but she's also pretty fond of them. I feed them more, but she thinks I'm feeding them to death.

Well, there was only one way to sort it – rock, paper, scissors… (There's a lesbian joke in there somewhere.) I won. Best of three? I won again. Best of five? Fine, I'll keep the bastards… I guess they'll keep me company once I move into my own place and I'm trying to get through those dark evenings when everything seems too

SCREWED UP, SLIMMED DOWN

overwhelming.

But hang on, what happens if there's an apocalypse?! We've spent many car rides planning our exact course of action if and when the zombies attack, but what happens now? Is our joint plan still in place or do I need to create a new one? What, on my own? That'll never work – we all know that the idiot who tries to go it alone dies first, strength in numbers and all that. I can just about survive my period every month, let alone a zombie apocalypse.

But it's not just zombies that we'd planned for, oh no, we had a structured procedure for every possible disaster: tsunamis, nuclear attacks, cybergeddon. The lot. I guess having to create a series of new SOS emergency plans will help fill up those lonely nights.

I've also got a new job (still in marketing). I didn't mention it before because work, ya know? Gross. It's based in Hove and I've got two weeks off in between jobs, the first week I'll still be living in Haywards Heath with Cat, but the second week will be in my new flat. Alone.

Do I want to spend my last week with Cat bursting into tears every time I see the boxes labelled 'Cat's' and 'Jenna's'? No, I shitting well don't. Well, there is only one thing for me to do: jump on a plane and go on a solo self-care holibobs to Spain.

Yes, I'm one of those dicks who says holibobs. Deal with it...

CHAPTER 19

SPAIN WILL DELAY MY PAIN

If I'm going to fall apart over my breakup, then the very least I can do is do it while sipping a cocktail by the pool and getting a sexy tan. Self. Bloody. Care. So that's why I've come here to Majorca, the home of the man with the sexiest left bicep, Rafael Nadal.

The night before I left, I cried myself to sleep. I was lonely as Cat was busy painting in the lounge. I could've gone through and hugged her or asked her to come to bed, but soon it's just going to be me and she's not going to be there, so I need to get used to being lonely again. Also, she's really enjoying her painting and it's not fair for me to disturb her just to make me feel better. She's painting me a paint-by-numbers picture of Baby Yoda for my new flat that I've found just outside of Hove.

This is my first holiday on my own in 10 years, and I thought that going on holiday on my own would mean that people would stare a lot. But actually, there aren't that many Germans here… That's a joke. There's bloody hundreds of them.

Before I came away Cat gave me two rules: one, don't

SCREWED UP, SLIMMED DOWN

get drunk and go for a midnight swim in the sea. And two, talk to people. Like, other people, like, other human beings. Communicate with them verbally and not just with their dogs.

But approaching strangers can be hard; also I've got a resting bitch face which means that if I'm not gurning at you then it'll look like I'm giving you a really dirty look. There's no in-between... I practised my 'approachable' face before I left my hotel room and went down to dinner on the first night, but it just gave me face-ache so I stopped it after two minutes.

I'd rather be lonely with a comfortable face, thanks.

The first day I meandered around the shops, picking up some typical Spanish items to take home with me, things like paella in a box, flick knives and penis bottle openers. Culture, darling, I'm all about it.

In terms of eating, I considered continuing with my intermittent fasting and 'Jenna's form of keto', but within seconds of seeing the breakfast buffet I thought, 'Bollocks, I'm on a self-care holiday, if I want Nutella for bloody breakfast, then I'll have Nutella for bloody breakfast.' So, yes, I *did* have Nutella for bloody breakfast because there's a giant (and I mean giant) jar of it with a pump. A pump... sod your tapas and paella, I'll just have a bowl. *squirts Nutella into a bowl*

At least the risk of me getting the squits here is low, what with the buffet being full of things like chips, pizza and ice cream (and that's just breakfast). When Cat and I went to Thailand a few years ago we both had a terrible dose of food poisoning from some prawns that we had in a restaurant where one of the waiters was a five-year-old child who ran around naked. We spent the next day sharing the toilet (again, that's a joke, we've never actually sat on the same toilet at the same time).

'I don't think I could love you any more,' I'd told Cat as I sat on the bathroom floor watching her sitting naked on the toilet, expelling liquids from both ends. We really *did* holiday well together.

But now I'm on a sad lonely holibobs on my own, I mean, my empowering solo vacation, hell yeah!

I took myself out on a date last night. I thought that, a) she'd pay and, b) the night would finish with a happy ending but unfortunately, *I* had to pay *and* I had to finish myself off at the end of the night. I've had dates like that before…

The date started at the hotel buffet, where I sat in my best shirt stuffing my face with chips while watching all the other diners. There was a couple who were both sitting on their phones, a couple who were well into their 60s and had clearly run out of conversation two decades ago and a really miserable couple who were just staring into the abyss while their kid threw food at their faces. Lonely on your own, or lonely together – I think I'd rather the former.

During my date I treated myself to a stupidly expensive piña colada at the beach bar before spending the rest of the evening sitting on the beach downing the cheap cans of beer that I'd bought in the supermarket.

As I sat on my own drinking my feelings, avoiding the heartache that was waiting for me back home, I watched as a group of young Spanish people canoodled and danced around their beach BBQ. Their positivity was infectious.

> **Earl:** Do you think that these Spanish women also have really dark hairy bums, like you?
> **Me:** Probably.
> **Earl:** Nah, they're probably smooth and bare, like a woman should be. It's only you who has the arse of an ape.
> **Me:** At least the hair keeps my arse warm.
> **Wanda:** Yes, Jenna!! You're turning what you think is a negative into a positive, this is great!!
> **Earl:** Thankfully no one else will ever see your hairy arse again, what with your new and permanent spinster status.

SCREWED UP, SLIMMED DOWN

I stumbled back to my hotel in a drunken haze, smiling and laughing to myself and taking selfies with every Rafael Nadal poster I saw along the way.

The next day, once the hangover had softened and my beer fear-induced anxiety had stopped screaming, I plonked myself next to the pool and began reading my Martina Me-love-some-pavlova tennis book. Suddenly, one of the jazzed-up children's entertainers came on the speakers.

'Hola, hello, guten tag, olé! Ladies and gentlemen, we will soon be playing water polo in the pool, olé! All those who want to join in, make your way to the shallow end. OLÉ!' I tilted my book down and looked at the pool. I wanted to play water polo. I *always* want to play water polo when I'm on my holidays but I never *ever* do because I'm too scared about what people will think of me.

Look, there's a fat idiot woman who can't play water polo trying to have fun and play water polo while she's on holiday!! The audacity…

'I want to play water polo,' I mumbled to myself while watching the massive bald blokes make their way to the shallow end. I closed my book.

Earl: What the hell do you think you're doing?
Me: I'm going to play water polo.
Wanda: Yay, sports, let's go!
Earl: But everyone's going to think you're an absolute twit.
Wanda: Who cares what they think? Fun activities, yay, let's do it!
Earl: You'll regret it.
Wanda: You will only regret things that you didn't do. Now, go and play water polo!
Earl: Don't come crying to me when you get hit in the face with the ball and everyone laughs…

SCREWED UP, SLIMMED DOWN

Ladies and gentlemen, I went to play water polo. I was crap, I hardly ever got the ball thrown to me, one guy shoved me out of the way and I was a massive hindrance to my entire team. But… It… Was… Fun. I totally forgot about the breakup, about what other people thought of me and I was just in the game, playing. It was fantastic.

I left my comfort zone and it paid off. So, the goal for the next chapter of my life (which is just a few days away, shit) is to get myself out of my comfort zone more and more. I've made a good start on it, what with going on holiday on my own, playing water polo and wearing my 'approachable' face for those two whole minutes.

I fly home tomorrow and I know what's waiting for me. Hell. My world is about to fall apart. But at least I can now go through it with a sexy tan.

Well, as sexy a tan as four days in Majorca can get you…

CHAPTER 20

DEATH WOULD'VE BEEN EASIER

I've left her family WhatsApp group. This might seem trivial, but it sucks. Hard. It was the day before we moved out of our flat and earlier I took myself to the bedroom, sat on the bed and wrote out my goodbye text (always one for the dramatics).

'I love you all very much and you'll always be like family to me. I'm going to leave this group for obvious reasons but I hope I get to see you all again one day, even you Rachel [Cat's intimidating sister] xxx' And then I exited the group.

Hot tears fell from my eyes as I sat there alone on the bed. I've never had much family, and because my parents broke up when I was young I've never really felt a part of a big warm family unit. But it was different with Cat's lovely family.

Her family is full of typical Scots in the sense that they're friendly, loud and enjoy calling me an English twat. But they welcomed me with open arms (well, mostly, once the Catholic ones had gotten over the whole gay thing), but here I was cutting them out of my life.

A few minutes later Cat came into the bedroom, tears already pouring down her face, arms spread out ready to hug me. She had just read the message. She sat on the bed and held me as we sobbed together.

This feels like a death. A proper big ugly shitting death, but one that I've brought on myself. Jesus, well done Jenna. Bonus points for sodding everything up.

CHAPTER 21

LESS FAT, MORE SAD

I'm now halfway through my transformation year, from fat, depressed lesbian to just a lesbian/super-hot babe. But let's have a look at where I am in terms of my goals.

Am I still fat? Yes, but I'm *less* fat. I've lost one and a half stone and the whole weight loss thing has recently picked up a lot more momentum compared to the beginning of the year when I didn't really have a clue what I was doing. Intermittent fasting and 'Jenna's form of keto' is working bloody wonders (when I'm actually sticking to it and not on holiday eating Nutella soup).

What's keeping me motivated? Well, apart from the fact that if I stop I might actually break, I have a couple of friends who are motivating me in different ways. Louise is motivating me with the fitness. She constantly kicks my arse at badminton and due to my competitive nature I hope to one day get revenge and crush her soul, I mean... crush her at badminton.

My other newly made friend, Jamie (who used to live next door to us in Haywards Heath and now lives down in Hove), is motivating me with the whole physical look thing. Jamie and her future wife, Josie, are two very fashionable lesbos who constantly serve up these incredible looks. Jamie's constantly asking me what I'm wearing, so I now have to make an effort with what I put on my body and not just throw on anything that fits.

Being focused on my looks is slightly shallower than I'm used to, because I've always been told that you shouldn't put too much effort into your appearance because that's vain. But Jamie is showing me that *actually* the way you dress and show up in the world gives you confidence and makes you feel good. And I just want to feel good, bbz.

'So stop wearing these huge black tents and serve a bloody look, Jenna.' Her exact words.

What are my goals for the next six months? Well, apart from the whole getting over my first breakup and not killing myself thing, I've signed up for a tennis tournament at the tennis club, which is now five minutes down the road from me rather than 35.

I'm in the semi-finals already (because I'm just *that* good and definitely not because only four women entered), so if I want to have a chance of getting into the final then I've got to work more on my physical health and fitness.

In terms of the goal for my mental health, that's not going to be as easy as strapping on a pair of trainers and waving a tennis racket around.

There's not really an end goal with the mental health, apart from reaching nirvana and true enlightenment, but as I've just completely ballsed up everything in my life, I guess I'll say that getting through the next six months without driving into a wall will be an absolute miracle.

Four days ago I moved away from the hell that was Haywards Heath and into a delightful little town next to Hove where the 4x4s outnumber the people. Yes, I know, I've chosen to live in another Tory stronghold, what can I say? I vote Labour but love living in a Tory area – the gardens are better kept.

The day Cat and I moved out was the worst day of my life. I had wanted to move out of Haywards Heath five minutes after we'd moved in, and when the day finally arrived it wasn't full of the elation that I was expecting. It was full of tears, anxiety and existential terror. Me and Cat are no more. My person for over eight years is no longer there by my side. And it was *my decision*.

Me: What have I done?
Earl: You're totally fucked.
Wanda: It might hurt now, but it will make sense for both of you in the future.
Earl: Nothing will ever make sense again. Perhaps it would be best to break into NASA and blast yourself straight into the void.
Wanda: You will get through this.
Earl: But you're going to die one day anyway, so it doesn't really matter if you do get through it.

On moving day my dad came round to see me in my new flat on his way back from visiting my brother in Dorset. He was very sweet and kept hugging me. Probably because after spending a weekend at my brother's house, he now realises what an absolute angel I am.

I didn't know how much I needed someone else on the day my world fell apart. I thought I could just struggle through it on my own, I thought I didn't need anyone. Other people can't be relied upon, so best to just rely on yourself. But *actually*, I really needed my dad that day and he was there for me.

When Cat and I left our flat in Haywards Heath for the last time on breakup day, we hugged for what was never going to be long enough. We cried into each other arms before sheepishly getting into our own cars and driving away, both of us torn between wanting the hell to be over and wanting to delay our parting for as long as possible.

Cat drove away first and I was in my car behind her when we both got caught at a red traffic light around the corner. When the light turned green she was going to turn left and I was going to turn right and as we waited for the red light to change I cried my eyes out in despair. I frantically wiped away the tears which were flooding my view of the woman in the car in front – my sweet darling.

As the lights turned from red to amber and then to green I stuck my hand out of the window and made the shape of half a love heart with my fingers – something I always used to do whenever I was leaving the flat, to which she would then do the same and we'd put our half hearts together to make a full heart. Cat stuck her hand out of the window and made half a love-heart shape with her fingers as her car slowly turned left.

Driving as slow as I possibly could, I watched as her car got smaller and smaller in my rear-view mirror, my hand still up out of the window in its half-love-heart shape. I never wanted to bring it down.

My deepest wish for this breakup is that I get to a place where I'm either back with Cat where we're both happy together and there's no more mental health bollocks tormenting my mind. *Or*, I'm not back with her, but we're both really happy being without each other romantically. She'll always be my best friend and my person, though – well, I hope so…

Have I had a panic attack every day since that awful breakup day? Yes, of course I have, darling, the demons haven't given me a sodding break. But I've got a fresh prescription of propranolol and Jamie has been texting me on the daily with self-care mantras, so luckily, my head isn't in the oven *quite* yet.

CHAPTER 22

FEELINGS SUCK...

July

What have I done? Holy shit... I can't do life on my own. Who am I without Cat? Who is Jenna? Who *is* she? WHO IS SHE? I don't know and I'm meant to *be* her! Christ, this is shit. Who knew breakups suck so hard? Apparently everyone, but I didn't have a bloody clue.

Even my usual 10-minute daily meditation isn't helping get rid of this sadness. Damn you, Eckhart Tolle.

I start my new job next week. I HATE jobs, even the best of them are tedious. Plus this new job is forcing me to go into an office three days a week, which is going to be a *nightmare* considering I've not been in an office for over four years. Getting up before 8 am? Working face-to-face with the office knobheads? Smiling and pretending that I'm enjoying my job and not dying inside at what a thorough waste of time the whole work thing is? I don't think I'll be able to cope.

And now Cat won't be there to help me cope... How *will* I cope? Eugh, too much coping to do.

Earl: The old head-in-the-oven thing looks tempting now, doesn't it?

Wanda: You can do this, I believe in you.
Earl: And I believe you'll have a panic attack within the first three hours of your new job.
Me: Thanks for the support.
Earl: Sorry, I take that back.
Me: Good, thank you.
Earl: You'll have one in the first *two* hours.

This week I've started binge-eating in the evenings and there may or may not have been a few nights where I've used alcohol to suppress all these stupid feelings. Feelings suck, don't they? Who knew feelings suck so bad? Yes, I know, everyone knows that breakups and feelings suck. Well, this is news to me. NEWS, I tell you!

Cat and I have been having video calls recently (we're both incredibly lonely and missing each other desperately) and they always end the same – both of us crying and me feeling so guilty at what I've put us through that I want to go into my bathroom, grab my razor and cut myself. Bad Jenna. You've screwed everything up and hurt the most amazing person in your life, the one person who actually loves/d you and you truly cocked it up.

Maybe I deserve to suffer. God, no, I take that back. That sounds a bit too 'victimy'.

'You will feel better, darling. It just takes a while. It will get one per cent better each day, keep going mate xx' Jamie texted me tonight before I got into bed. I'll wake up to another damp pillow in the morning. From my tears, not anything sexual; bitch, please, I'm FAR too emotional to come.

CHAPTER 23

DON'T ASK THE THERAPIST ABOUT HER VAGINA

After my previous therapist paid more attention to his clipboard than to me, I decided to change therapists, which is thoroughly annoying because now I have to tell my whole life story to yet *another* person.

I wish there was a way that I could upload my entire life right up until this point onto a USB stick and then give it to my new therapist so that she could download it and bing-bang-bong – be all caught up without me having to regurgitate everything.

When I first went into her office today I was greeted by a cute little room with two small electric fans, a patterned rug and an uncomfortable-looking two-seater sofa in front of the window. It was a sofa that had clearly been bought so that people don't get too comfortable. I reckon that's why she got it, so that her clients don't overrun on time. OK, maybe I should stop psychoanalysing my psychotherapist.

My new therapist is a very smiley kind-looking woman in her mid 40s. She sported a short blonde bob, an interesting combination of gold necklaces and a very fashionable jumpsuit.

'Hello, please take a seat,' she said, pointing to the rock disguised as a sofa. She plopped herself down on a matching chair opposite me, except that *her* chair had one of those special doughnut cushions that you sit on. I always thought those cushions were for women who had recently undergone some sort of vaginal rejuvenation treatment. (No, I didn't ask whether this was the case, I thought I'd save asking her about her vagina until we knew each other better.)

I told her all about what was happening with my breakup, about my long and arduous history with depression and how I'm very close to having a full-on breakdown.

'OK, so which bit do you want to focus on first?' she asked as calmly as one can ask a question that is basically, 'Which piece of this absolute horror show shall we tackle first?'

'Well, I'm used to feeling like a sack of shit with the depression, but I think that me being close to a breakdown is related to the breakup. So, I'd like to focus on the breakup stuff first, please,' I said, staring at the small electric fan on the floor next to my feet, which was providing zero relief from the summer heat.

After I told her all about what had happened with Cat, she paused, tilted her head and thought for a moment.

'It sounds like you've done the kindest thing for both of you. You clearly couldn't have stayed in a relationship that was stuck, so by you ending it, you've given both of you the opportunity to move forward,' she said, using her hands a lot for extra emphasis.

Wanda: See, I told you you've done the best thing for both of you. It sucks now, but it'll be worth it in the end.
Earl: So basically you've paid someone £50 to tell you what Wanda has already told you? Hahahahahahahaha!

SCREWED UP, SLIMMED DOWN

Idiot.

'I feel so alone and unwanted, and those feelings, mixed with the feelings of guilt over the breakup and anxiety about starting a new life in a town where I don't really know anyone that well is causing me to nearly lose it completely,' I told her.

Earl: Fix that, bitch.

She glanced at the clock on the little side table next to me. We had 15 minutes left.

'What you've done is incredibly brave, Jenna. Incredibly brave. You need to recognise that and be kind to yourself. You're going through a huge stage in your life where you're sorting out your mental health, you're putting yourself first by leaving a relationship that wasn't working, and you're starting afresh somewhere new, which although seems terrifying, is a great opportunity to start again, as the new you. So while we're not going to sort all of this out straight away, I want you to start by being gentle with yourself.' She pointed to the clock briefly. 'We've only got a few minutes left so we'll pick this up next week, but let's imagine that this journey that we're both about to go on together is like taking off the backpack of bricks that you've been lugging around for years, unzipping it and taking each of the bricks out, one by one. The bricks represent your past traumas, and slowly what we'll do in these sessions is take out a brick, talk about why you've been keeping it in there and we'll sort it out so that you don't have to carry around that brick anymore.'

I smiled at her. I liked this theory a lot.

'What we'll also do is have a look at your beliefs and whether they're still serving you. I like to explain this in the form of a card game. You've got your cards in your hand and you're keeping them close, but what we're actually going to do is put your cards down on the table, have a look at them and decide if we still want these particular cards. The cards represent your beliefs. So perhaps there's a card that represents Cat and the belief that "I must keep her happy or I'm a bad person".'

Wow, she's understood me *really* quickly.

'But does that belief serve you anymore? If we questioned this belief, would you still want to keep this card in your hand?'

'No, I wouldn't. It's not my job to make her happy and if I can't even make myself happy, how can I make someone else happy? She has to do it for herself and I need to do it for myself,' I said quickly without thinking or letting Earl slip into my mind to tell me that, yes, I must keep Cat happy and I'm a failure for not being able to save her.

'Exactly. That's fantastic that you're already able to see that.' She beamed.

Wow, progress after just one session. Incredible. I have such high hopes for these therapy sessions.

I wonder if she's thinking, 'Shit, I need to make sure that Jenna doesn't progress *too* quickly or she won't need as many sessions.' I guess therapists must constantly struggle with the dilemma of wanting to help their clients so that they find the sessions useful and keep coming back, but not wanting to help them *so* much that they're cured and then no longer need the sessions anymore.

Earl: Lol, 'cured', she's not *that* good.

CHAPTER 24

I'M NO LONGER OBESE

I've got some very important news to share: I'm no longer obese! I haven't been 'just overweight' for over nine years, so it's a momentous day indeed! The BMI chart (Bollocks Medical Index) says that if your BMI score is over 30 then you're obese and *mine* is now 29.9, aka, Skinny bloody Malinky.

After I celebrated by dancing around my bathroom naked, I Googled what my score would need to be in order to be just a 'normal' weight and it said that I'd actually need to have been dead for five years before I can reach that goal.

I can't see myself ever getting down to a 'normal weight', but there again, I never thought I'd get down to this weight – from 19 stone a few years ago to now 14 stone and 7 pounds. Who knows what the future holds? Hopefully a shitload of money and beautiful women who are obsessed with me, fingers crossed!

Since losing all this blubber I've noticed a few changes, some expected, some not. Basically, my arse has shrunk and my boobs have disappeared... My bottom used to be quite peachy, plump and round but now it's just totally flat, so either I'm going to have to start doing squats, or sit down less. And I don't really like the sound of either, if I'm honest.

Another new thing is that I've been checked out a few times. The other day I was in the park with my friend when a woman who was walking towards me started looking me up and down and smiling. When she went past, I turned to see if she was still looking AND SHE WAS! Still got it! (Did I ever have it? Well, that's not really for me to decide.) Not only am I now a Large in clothing size, but I'm also being objectified by strangers #lifegoals.

Something else that's new physically is that now I've got definition in places that I didn't realise you could get definition. E.g. my thighs no longer resemble a pair of corn dogs, as they now feature lines to show the separation between my excellent muscles and the large lump of fat that's still very much there.

Unfortunately, not all changes have been good… Since losing weight I've… God, this is difficult to write… I've been wearing more… colour. I know, I know.

'But Jenna, you're the lesbian Johnny Cash, the woman in black, the gay Grim Reaper!' I know! But now that I can wear clothes to actually look good and not just cover up my naked hairy flesh, I'm experimenting with all the colours of the rainbow. (Read: dark green and navy.)

One actual negative change since losing weight is that I can no longer get away with calling myself a 'person of girth'. Nope, can't get away with it. Nor can I make fat jokes anymore, and for years my comedy has been based purely on, a) how fat I am and, b) how gay I am. Now, I'm just stuck with gay jokes. It's like I'm losing my identity. God, what if this weight loss thing triggers some kind of chemical change within me and I turn straight? *Runs to McDonald's immediately* (lol, OK, 'runs' – I think we both know I mean 'drives without putting a bra on').

In two months' time, I'm going to America for a fortnight and I plan to lose another stone before I jet off on the big old American road trip. Actually, it's not technically a 'road trip', it's just a 'trip' because Americans drive on the other side of the road and we're going to Denver, New Orleans and Miami so we need to fly between destinations and also, Jenna doesn't drive on the wrong side of the road.

That's right, I said 'we'. Who are you going on a two-week awesome holiday with, Jenna? Is it a new girlfriend? Is it your new bestie? No. It's Cat. People go on holiday with their exes just a few months after breaking up, don't they? Well, we booked it over a year ago and neither one of us are going to give up this holiday of a lifetime, so we're going on it. Together.

We have two months until we fly, so I need to fill that time by working out how the *hell* I'm going to get through it. It'll either be incredible or awful. Fingers crossed for the former.

CHAPTER 25

HOW TO WORK 9–5 AND NOT SHOOT YOURSELF IN THE FACE

I start my new job tomorrow. Ever since I joined the unforgiving world of work I have endured a series of very soul-destroying jobs. Though aren't *all* jobs soul-destroying? Yes, they are and I will not be convinced otherwise.

Will this new job be different from all the others I've tried? It seems unlikely… My disinterest in working for 'the system' (or in truth, anyone) started when I was a shitty little 15-year-old and I got my first paper round.

Unlike my friends' paper rounds, I was paid £30 a week rather than £12 because I did the job in my mother's name, so that I got paid the adult minimum wage. Is that good business acumen? Or is that fraud? If it's fraud, then I am of *course* joking. I would *never* do such a thing.

My paper round consisted of me packing the newspapers into a trolley, wheeling them down to the river, chain-smoking cigarettes and then finding a bin to dump them in before returning home to tell my mum how physically demanding having a paper round was. Is that illegal? If so, then I am of *course* joking. I would *never* do such a thing.

The way I conducted myself with my newspaper job really set the tone for how my work ethic and attitude towards employment would be throughout my life; somewhat reluctant (read: appalling).

After I graduated with a 2:1 in media studies (yes, it is a real degree), I went to live with my dad, something I hadn't done since I was two years old, when food, shelter and nightly baths were free of charge. But for some strange reason, this was not how it was going to go down now that I was 23. My dad told me that I had to go out and get a job to pay rent, buy my own food and put towards the water rates. I was distraught.

'We're on a bloody meter, don't you know?' he would shout upstairs as I ran my third bath of the day.

So after a few weeks of the laziest job-hunting you've ever seen, I got a job. How can people say that getting a job after uni is hard? I found it incredibly easy… Oh, except my graduate job wasn't my dream 'work for a magazine in London' job, it was a 'serve pizza to idiots while eating your feelings' job. A description that I have since had to take off my CV because apparently it gives employers the wrong idea about me. (Though I'm sure you'll agree that it actually gives employers the *right* idea about me.)

Being a waitress is, and I don't mean to be dramatic here, fucking horrendous. I don't think it's too preposterous to say that it would even turn Mother Theresa into a murderous maniac who would rather have root-canal treatment on every tooth in her head than serve in a restaurant. (If she were alive of course, though I imagine having root-canal treatment done when you've been dead for two decades is probably the only time it's bearable.)

Here's a typical exchange with a customer:

Me: Hello and welcome to Pizz—

SCREWED UP, SLIMMED DOWN

Customer: Got a table for 18?
Me: A table for 18?
Customer: Yeah.
Me: Have you made a booking?
Customer: No.
Me: No?
Customer: No.
Me: No?
Customer: Nah, we haven't booked.
Me: Oh, I see, so you've just impulsively decided that all 18 of you should go out for dinner on a Saturday night without booking?
Customer: Yeah.
Me: Fabulous.
Customer: So you got room for us?
Me: Absolutely, just bear with me while I push four tables together and then go and slit my wrists in the staff room
Customer: Great, cheers, love.

10 minutes later

Me: Are you ready to order, sir?
Customer: Yeah, I'll have the chicken and pineapple pizza, but instead of the chicken I'll have pepperoni, and instead of the pineapple I'll have mushrooms.
Me: …
Customer: And instead of the side salad, I'll have coleslaw.
Me: And instead of a plate would you like a bowl?
Customer: Excuse me?
Me: And instead of a knife and fork would you like two spoons?
Customer: You what?
Me: Nothing, sir, that's wonderful. And what can I get for you, madam?
Customer #2: Oh, just to let you know that I have a

SCREWED UP, SLIMMED DOWN

nut allergy.

Me: No problem. I'll make a note of that and let the chefs know.

Customer #2: I'm also gluten-free, lactose-free and a vegan.

Me: Right.

Customer #2: Also, little Theodore only likes anchovies on his pizza and Timmy is allergic to anything that casts a shadow.

Me: Well, fuck me sideways.

I don't know if you can tell from the above example, but I hated that job. Here's a piece of advice for you – if you're in a job you hate, quit! The threat of not being able to afford food, shelter and Nike trainers will hopefully motivate you enough to get a new job. Is that good advice? Probably not, but it's what I would do if I'd only listen to the bollocks/wisdom that comes out of my own mouth.

After two years of eating non-stop carbs and drinking like a sailor to numb the pain of working in hospitality, I finally escaped.

Growing up, my dream was to live and work in London. Ahhh, London Town, so shiny, so glamorous, so sexy. I imagined I would work 9–5, go out with friends in the evening and feel so horny for life. Cut to just five years after university and I finally landed my dream 'work for a magazine in London' job.

I sashayed into the large London building with hope, positivity and spunk. JENNA HAS ARRIVED!

Earl: Well, this job makes me want to kill myself.

Me: Same.

Earl: Will there ever be any hope again?

Me: I doubt it. I've got to run a report on our Twitter activity this afternoon.

Earl: Hopefully lunch will poison us both before we get to it.

SCREWED UP, SLIMMED DOWN

Me: Fingers crossed.

Eight hours later I crawled out of the building feeling drained, hopeless and all spunked out. JENNA HAS ESCAPED THE BUILDING AND WILL NOT BE RETURNING!

My dream job turned out to be boring, tedious and utterly ghastly, yet all my colleagues walked around like they were curing cancer or something. But in reality, they were working for a magazine that was so dull it made the *Financial Chronicle* look incredibly thrilling.

HOWEVER, there were free posh cupcakes in the canteen every other Friday, so swings and roundabouts…

It's funny, because I remember a time when I thought that coming out as a lesbian and being the only woman in an office full of men would be the worst thing about work. HA! Oh, young Jenna, you have much to learn. If you're gay – or indeed any other letter on the gay alphabet – don't worry about coming out at work or receiving prejudice, that's one of the more *tolerable* things about work. The worst bit is the actual work.

I quit that 'dream' job after a month, though how I lasted that long I've no idea, and I vowed never to remain in a job that made me feel so utterly dejected again. Cut to six years later and I've completely forgotten that I made that vow.

I believe that the world of employment contributes heavily to my depression, but to be fair, my depression probably makes it worse. But which came first? It's a chicken and egg thing. One has to go!

I'm hoping that my mission to vastly improve my depression will make work more sufferable. But there again, dealing with depression is a bit of a long old slog, so maybe if I want to feel better right now I should try quitting my job first and then see if that helps.

Christ, I start my new job tomorrow and I'm already thinking of quitting… #DreamEmployee.

CHAPTER 26

FILL UP MY POCKETS AND EMPTY OUT MY SOUL

I started my new job today. I won't tell you exactly how it went, I'll just tell you that two hours into the job I was sat on the toilet Googling 'How to quit the 9–5 and make money from writing'. It turns out that all jobs *are* mind-numbingly tedious. God, I hate being right all the time.

Since I tried the cold-water therapy a few months ago, I've still been having a cold shower in the morning and that helps me for maybe a few minutes, but soon afterwards the existential crisis creeps back in.

I realise now that it's my mental health that's making me hate work, because how unbearable does a job have to be for me to want to quit on the first day? It's got to be a bit of a shocker, right? I could be hired as Kate Winslet's personal masseuse and due to the crisis I'm going through right now, I'd probably still hate it. Though I imagine it would be slightly more bearable than my new job in marketing where I spent most of the day pretending to watch and care about the training videos they sat me in front of.

I called Cat during my lunch break and she made me

SCREWED UP, SLIMMED DOWN

feel so much better about the whole work thing. When I say 'lunch break' I just mean the time I spent away from my desk, because I'd already eaten all of the food I'd brought with me by 9:01 am. Intermittent fasting is going to be bloody impossible on the days I'm in the office…

During our call, Cat reminded me that this job is just my side hustle and that it's my writing and comedy videos that are my *main* thing. This 9–5 bullshit (actually it's 8:30–5 which is another bucket of bollocks) is just paying the bills.

'Also, the first few weeks at a new job are always a bit crap,' she said. Are they? Or are they meant to be the best bit of the job before it slowly takes its toll and begins to fill you with dread and despair? 'Just plod along in the job and when you get home do some awesome writing and then give me a video call.'

Oh yeah, Cat and I are still video-calling every day. That's what couples normally do after they break up, isn't it? They're meant to still be in constant contact and sending each other cute little love bear gifs before they go to sleep, right?

It might not be the normal thing that people do, and it might make things difficult in the long run, but right now having this closeness to Cat is helping me get through these cripplingly lonely nights. I don't know what I'd do if she wasn't there on the other end of the phone. Me, codependent? No, I won't hear it.

……

I'm now two weeks into my new job. Has it gotten any better? No. Have I had three panic attacks at work? Yes. Is the office dull and boring and when I'm having a bad mental health day (which at the moment, is every single day), is it difficult for me to stop crying in the toilets? Yes. Enough with the questions, please.

I had a meeting with my boss today about going down

to working twice a week in the office rather than three times because I'm really struggling to be around other human beings. I may have also dropped the term 'mental health' into our conversation, which I was hoping would guarantee a 'yes' response. However, although she said that she was fine with it, she asked her boss (think David Brent from *The Office*, but more dull) and he said no. I then told her about the panic attack that I'd literally just had in the toilet before the meeting, and she said she'd ask her boss again.

Thanks to the small pot of money that I made on the flat in Haywards Heath, I can afford to quit my job and focus on my writing for about five months, but that would be all of my savings gone and also the news today is full of doom about an impending recession. Perhaps I should just spend the money on a little camper-van and live my van life fantasy instead.

> **Earl:** You can't quit your job, there's a recession coming.
> **Wanda:** It'll never be the right time to quit, you've just got to go for it!
> **Earl:** You'll end up homeless.
> **Me:** No, I won't.
> **Earl:** Or worse…
> **Me:** Worse?
> **Earl:** Living back with your parents.

CHAPTER 27

HANNAH BROKE MY HEART

I've found a way to help get me through the days when I have to go into the office: I go to the local park at lunchtime and sit opposite the tennis courts, where I watch a very hot blonde tennis coach teach retired people how to play tennis while wearing very tight short shorts. That's the coach wearing the very tight shorts, not the retired people, I've no idea what they were wearing – they could've been dressed as Hitler and I wouldn't have noticed. Hot blondes playing tennis will make my working day go that little bit smoother.

Yesterday, after another long day of crying in the work toilets, I made my way to the station to catch the train home. As I stepped onto the platform I saw a familiar face in the distance. Was it her? No, it couldn't be… She still lives in Devon… It was her! Standing just five metres away from me on Hove train station was Hannah (my best friend from school who I fell in unrequited love with).

I laughed to myself when I realised it was her. I haven't seen her since I was 18 years old, and back then I would've done *anything* for Hannah. She was my world, my happiness depended on her and her alone. (Again, me, codependent? I've told you, I WON'T HEAR IT!) And

126

here she was standing on the same platform as me, the woman who helped me realise that I was gay.

I feel like I've just brushed past the whole lesbian thing. So, yes, I am a lesbian, and like I said at the beginning of this book, it is *still* the most interesting thing about me.

When I first met Hannah I was 14 years old, but at that time I still didn't know that I was a lesbian. Sure, there had been signs, but like with the rules of grammar in this book, I completely ignored them.

At the age of nine I was blissfully unaware that cutting out pictures of Kate Winslet and putting them into a photo frame was an odd thing for a young girl to do.

This pattern of 'odd behaviour' continued when I put a poster of Geri Halliwell wearing a small army outfit on my wall, and my brother told me that girls aren't supposed to have pictures of women on their walls. This was a deeply concerning time, because not only did I find myself really liking the look of Geri in those small camouflage shorts, but it also put into question whether or not Sporty Spice was still my favourite.

This period of wanting to look at women continued to grow as I found myself 'accidentally' switching over to the Living TV channel where I came across a programme called *The L Word*. Hmm, what on earth could the 'L' stand for, I wondered…

Of course young Jenna knew EXACTLY that the 'L' stood for. The first scene I watched of the programme showed Bette and Tina (two 30-something lesbians) getting it on in the kitchen, and I was *disgusted*. Two old ladies getting it on… gross! I quickly changed the channel and tried to shake off the dirty feeling that had come over me. Eighteen years on and I've rewatched that scene, many, MANY times, with a more open-minded and, let's say, positive type of reaction.

I moved around a lot as a kid, and as I sat down in my first English class in my new secondary school in Devon, the girl next to me introduced herself.

SCREWED UP, SLIMMED DOWN

'Hi, I'm Lauren and everyone says that I got off with a horse, but I didn't. That's my best friend over there, her name is Hannah.'

'Which one?'

'The girl with the pink fluffy coat on the back of her chair.'

'Oh... cool.'

That pink fluffy coat was just the beginning. Cut to a few years later and I was self-harming in the bath while listening to Celine Dion medleys because of that girl with the pink fluffy coat. But I'm jumping forward too fast.

From our first meeting, Hannah and I were paired up in most of our classes and we got on even better than Emily and I had all those years ago back in primary school. Except this time there was no risk of Hannah leaving me to join the cool kids, because she *was* the cool kid.

Hannah made me feel alive. I woke up, I thought of Hannah, I went to bed, I thought of Hannah, I took a dump in a crowded school toilet, I thought of how much bullying I would get after I stepped out of the bathroom stall, *and* I thought of Hannah. I could *not* stop thinking of Hannah.

That was when the puberty-riddled Jenna started wearing even more black: black trousers, black makeup, black mood. The young lesbian Johnny Cash was born.

Hannah and I did everything together, and it was during this time that I started taking long solitary walks in the evening to the beach (while chain-smoking a packet of 20 menthol Superkings) to work out what all these weird feelings were that I was having.

As I stared out into the wild sea... (Was it wild? Gawd knows, but it adds more drama to this bit.) As I stared out into the fiery, raging sea, I realised that I was in love with this girl, I realised that I wasn't straight and I realised that I had a terrible smoking habit for a 15-year-old.

Acceptance is the first step in knowing you've got a problem. Not that being a lesbian is a problem (well, that depends on who you ask), but in this case the whole being-in-love-with-my-best-friend thing was the problem.

I didn't know how to handle all the love, puberty and hatred that was swimming around my chubby little body. So, after my long beachy walks I would have a bath and then take a razor to my arm. Celine Dion's 'It's All Coming Back to Me Now' would be playing on my phone and I'd cry hysterically while I cut myself. It must be the most emo thing you've *ever* heard (although, I'm pretty sure that most emos aren't into Celine Dion).

Yes, self-harming hurts, but nothing hurts quite like the morning after when you have to peel your pyjama sleeves off of the self-harming scabs that they've fused themselves to.

Looking back now, I can see that this is where my journey with depression really began. Sure, I had previously dipped my foot in the pool of shit during primary school what with all the bullying that was happening, but it seemed that now I had jumped right in. Headfirst. Totally naked.

I feel at this point I have to make a very serious and important disclaimer – if anyone is reading this and considering self-harm as some sort of cure for unwanted feelings, it's not. It will *not* make you feel better, it will just hurt you and everyone around you, not to mention your arm. Instead, why not reach out to your doctor, get some therapy or read one of the millions of amazing self-help books? Trust me, they're better than any Celine-Dion-induced self-harming session.

It wasn't until I was 18 that I finally told Hannah that I was in love with her, and by that point I was already filled with more hurt and emotion than you could shake a stick at. Though why you'd shake a stick at it is beyond me. Does that do anything? I'll have to try it…

Did Hannah, with her long hair, makeup and attraction to men, like me back? No, she did not. I know, what a shocker.

SCREWED UP, SLIMMED DOWN

Let me assure you that anyone who says that us gays brainwash people to join our cult is talking bollocks. Despite all my efforts, I just couldn't scout this girl to play for my team for love nor money. Not that I offered money.

Here's what *should* have happened when I told her that I loved her:

Me: I love you.
Her: I'm straight.
Me: Is there any way that you could fall in love with a chubby little emo goth girl like me?
Her: Yeah, probably.
Me: Great!
Her: In fact, we should get together now and have all the mad lesbian sex. Then we'll get married, adopt nine rescue dogs and become militant recycling warriors.
Me: *pulls her in for a big snog*

Here's what *actually* happened when I told her I loved her:

Me: I love you.
Her: I'm straight.
Me: Is there any way that you cou—
Her: No.
Me: But I…
Her: I said no.
Me: Oh.
Her: Don't ever contact me again.

Up until this year, that was the most difficult thing that I have ever gone through (before I was introduced to the world of utility bills and mortgage repayments, of course). Unrequited love is so much fun, especially when you're overflowing with hormones and your BMI is shooting up more than Ewan McGregor in that film where he swims in

SCREWED UP, SLIMMED DOWN

the toilet.

So, once I'd finally worked out that I was a shirt-and-trousers type of woman, it was time to tell everyone about it.

As my parents separated when I was just a fat little toddler, I decided to tell them about my lesbian-ness separately. It seemed only fair that if I get double the presents for birthdays and Christmas I should have to endure double the coming out.

I told my mum when I was 16 and it went something like this:

Me: Mum, you know the boy that I said I was in love with called Darren?
Mum: Yes.
Me: Well, Darren is a girl. Called Hannah.
Mum: …
Me: I'm a lesbian.

That was when she got up off the sofa and hugged me. It was the most boringly perfect coming out ever. When I told my brother he just laughed and called me a lezza.

After telling my mum and brother, I was ready to tell my dad… five years later.

Me: Dad, I've got something to tell you.
Dad: Move, you're blocking the TV.
Me: I don't really know how to say this.
Dad: What is it?
Me: I'm bisexual. (I thought that telling him I was bisexual would somehow be less of a blow than me being a full-blown gay.)
Dad: Oh, ahahahahahahaha.
Me: It was really difficult for me to tell you.
Dad: Really? Oh yeah, I've seen it on TV when people make a big thing about it. It doesn't matter to me.
Me: Great!

Dad: Is that it?
Me: Yes.
Dad: Good. Now shut up 'cos I want to watch the rest of this.

It had been 14 years since that horrendously turbulent time with Hannah, but as I stood on the platform yesterday just a few steps away from her, I didn't even want to go and say hello. I just looked at her, smiled to myself and walked away down the platform. I didn't even bother to see if she got on my train.

I am 100 per cent over this woman, who at one point was my entire world and I would've died just to hold her hand.

Wanda: See, Jenna, there *is* hope for the future. One day you will be over Cat and this pain will be a distant memory. You've just got to go through this shitstorm first.
Me: I know, thanks bbz.

CHAPTER 28

NO STRINGS ATTACHED

August

Like the tennis superstar Emma Raducanu, I grew up in Bromley, South London, and I also did the exam to get into that posh all-girls school that she went to, but that's where the similarities end, because I failed the entry exam and I can't play tennis very well.

Without being too dramatic, the little tennis club down the road from me has saved my life. This little club and the people in it are the only things getting me through this crisis at the moment – well, *most* of the people there, anyway, obviously there are some *absolute* tennis-club-type people there, if you know what I mean (snobbish beyond belief and like to walk around like they've got a stick up their arse).

Now that I'm no longer obese (and I've been smoke-free for two years), I'm able to run around the court with so much more ease. I mean, it's still not the prettiest sight in the world, but I'm not huffing and puffing all over the place. This increase in my fitness ability is also keeping me focused on my weight-loss goals, which could have totally gone out the bollocking window because normally I like to binge my feelings away, but now I'm playing them away.

Yay, go me.

A month before Cat and I broke up, the tennis club sent everyone an email with a list of strict rules that everyone must follow: only expensive-looking cars are allowed to park near the front of the car park and can everyone please keep regional accents to a minimum. At the bottom of the email, it mentioned the up-and-coming summer club championships.

'There's a club championship tournament,' I told Cat.

'You should enter.'

'But I'm crap,' I told her as if this were the most obvious piece of information ever.

'No, you're not. You should enter.'

'But what if people think I'm a sad idiot for entering?' I asked.

'Why on earth would they think that? And also, who cares what other people think? You like playing tennis, go and play tennis. I'd love to come and watch you play a match,' she replied, smiling at me.

Now, as I go through the worst time in my life, a time when I have zero meaning and a billion tears, I have a tennis tournament to focus on. And I am DEADLY serious about it.

I'd booked in a couple of practice matches with some of my friends from the club to prepare me for my first match next week, and I haven't won any of the practice matches yet but I'm sure that's fine. Does Djokovic win *every* practice match that he plays? Yes, I imagine he probably does. Shit…

Tennis is a game of errors, which means that the person who messes up the most normally loses. Oh God, I'm going to lose miserably… It's probably time I started listening to what my tennis coach is actually telling me…

'Look at the ball! Get your racket back early! It's tennis, not badminton, stop doing drop shots! Why are you crying on the floor? Don't smash your racket against your face!'

My semi-final match is tomorrow and I am fully

SCREWED UP, SLIMMED DOWN

prepared; I've chosen the best sports bra to wear, the best shorts, t-shirt, pants, perfume, deodorant, the lot! And if *that* doesn't work then I guess I'll actually have to try and hit the ball back over the net, but that is at a *last* resort, what with my level being only slightly better than crap.

Jamie and Josie are coming to watch. Unfortunately, Cat can't make it as she's going to a day festival with her other friend, which is probably for the best because we're trying to make sense of this breakup and hanging out all the time isn't even slightly what the breakup blogs recommend.

> **Earl:** You're going to do terribly.
>
> **Me:** I might do terribly, but I will try my best.
>
> **Earl:** Which will be more embarrassing because if you *didn't* try and you lost then it's because you didn't try – but if you try your best and still lose then it's just because you're shit.
>
> **Wanda:** Whatever happens, you're putting yourself out there and you'll have fun!
>
> **Me:** Thanks, Wanda.
>
> **Wanda:** Senior Wimbledon awaits!
>
> **Me:** Who are you calling senior? I'm 32!

CHAPTER 29

I AM NOT THE LESBIAN NADAL

The tennis tournament is over and now I have nothing to be fit and healthy for *cracks open a can of lager*. I'm joking; please, I've still got a very wobbly belly and a 'Medium' size goal t-shirt to fit into.

I know this might come as a shock, but I didn't win the tennis match… I *did* play well in the second set, though, it's just that I needed the first set to figure out how the hell to play tennis. And then once I'd realised that and I was understanding what my opponent doesn't like (when I hit drop shots), I started winning more points. Maybe I should ignore my coach more often…

When Jamie and Josie turned up to watch I saw that Josie was wearing a white t-shirt that said 'Go Jenna, Go!' I finally have my own support group! Woo hoo! My fan club sat on the grass next to the tennis court and cheered me on.

I lost the first set 0-6, which for those of you who don't know how the tennis scoring system works, is not the *best* score. But I did lose the second set 4-6, which is basically amazing and almost the best score you can get for a set and still lose it (unless you go to a tiebreak, or go to 5-7, but we didn't, so stop banging on about it).

SCREWED UP, SLIMMED DOWN

Once the match was over, I felt my body relax – all these weeks of anxiety and training were finally over. Yes, I lost, but during that second set I'd really tried to problem-solve why I was losing so spectacularly and I managed to win those four games, sooooo, really, I did fantastic and you should be proud of me.

'Shall we go for some lunch somewhere?' Jamie asked as we walked out of the tennis club.

Earl: Wtf? She wants to go out for lunch?
Me: I know! What the hell?
Earl: But that means we have to be social for longer than we had mentally prepared for.
Me: I know… I don't really have an excuse to get out of it. Also, I don't really *want* to get out of it. That's a weird feeling…
Wanda: Fantastic! Go and have a celebratory lunch with your two friends who have not only helped you through your breakup but also have been your fan club this morning!
Me: Yeah, I guess so…
Wanda: Plus, you've earned a big fat burger.
Earl & Me: This is very true…

I don't know what it is about rubbery, dry pub burgers, but they just don't have the appeal that they used to… I used to LOVE mopping up my pool of ketchup and mayo with my burger, no matter how absolutely inedible it was. But since I've been eating healthier and losing weight, I actually don't think it's worth the calories. Who have I become??

Me and the girls (ooo, get me, 'me and the girls', as if I've become one of those people that just casually have lunch with friends on the weekend) had a lovely lunch (apart from the crap burger), and I felt for the first time in ages like a 'normal' non-twattish person who has friends.

Maybe I *am* normal after all… Oh God, I hope not. I

like being weird. Weird but normal, let's go for that.

CHAPTER 30

SELF-WORTH WITH NEXT-DAY DELIVERY

How the hell am I meant to live on my own? I mean, I have two guinea pigs so I'm not *totally* on my own, but they've told me that I can't count on them for shit. The only thing I *can* count on them for is to actually... shit.

I've been living on my own for two months now and I thought it would be easy. Well, easier than this, anyway. But it seems to be getting harder.

At the beginning of the year I was in a relationship, I had exciting plans to move to Edinburgh, I owned a flat and had rooms full of wonderful memories. And now, here I am just outside of Hove, in a rented flat on my own that's swarming with earwigs thinking, who the hell am I? It's me thinking that, not the earwigs. I don't know what they're thinking. Probably 'Why does this fat human keep sucking us up with her Dyson?'

I keep checking my phone waiting for someone to text, anyone to prove that I'm not alone. Anyone to prove that I am worthy. *Am* I worthy? What is self-worth? Do I have it? Can I buy it on Prime with next-day delivery?

I had another panic attack last night. Another night of the demons screaming at me, telling me that I can't cope on my own, that everything is bad and waa waa waa.

During the panic attack I was thinking about what I should do with all the plans that Cat and I had. We were going to drive the North Coast 500, go to New York for a long weekend, camper-van around New Zealand, go to Vietnam, Laos and Cambodia. But who do I do that with now? On my own? What?! But life is so scary on your own!

We had plans to do *everything* together and now apparently we can't even share an Amazon account – she texted me recently saying that we have to stop sharing all of our streaming accounts. I guess I'll have to set up my own one, especially if I want to buy that self-worth on Amazon.

When I first started living on my own it was quite exciting, having everything I wanted *exactly* where I wanted it. Being able to watch as much bloody tennis as I want to without feeling an ounce of guilt – the guinea pigs can't see the TV from their cage so they don't get a say, not that they would anyway. That's a lie – if they wanted to watch something else we would watch something else.

At least living on my own also means that I don't have to flush down my wee wees, because you know how the old saying goes: if it's yellow, let it mellow, if it's brown, flush it down. If any future girlfriend is reading this, then *of course* I flush down my wee wees, I'm not an animal – if any future *wife* is reading this, then of course you'll know that I *am* an animal, but I will also do as I'm told and flush down my wee wees.

Everything is reminding me of Cat at the moment, and I guess it doesn't help that I've been wearing my wedding ring on my middle finger and kissing it when I need something to comfort me. Which, at the moment, is a million times a day. Christ, does that sound sad?

SCREWED UP, SLIMMED DOWN

Earl: More than you could ever possibly know.

The main issue that has made this breakup suck super hard is that Cat and I were ridiculously codependent on each other. Although, I always thought that *she* was more codependent than me – when people used to ask her what makes her happy she would reply with, 'Whatever makes Jenna happy', but since we parted I've realised how codependent I was, and *still* am.

I can't make myself feel validated, no, no, I need someone else to do that. When I'm having a panic attack or I can't get out of bed or the shower because I can't stop crying and am drowning in despair, I need Cat or Jamie, just someone to say it's going to be OK.

Cat and I had been texting each other with cute little messages (in between the 'make sure Jenna isn't walking into the sea' messages). Our texts were somewhere in between girlfriends and best friends. It was helping me because I know that I don't *have* her anymore, but also, I kind of *do* still have her – just as a best friend.

Until last week.

'I noticed you're being a bit different,' I texted her after the third message in a row from her that had zero warmth or kisses.

'I am a little, I'm trying to live without you and find out who I am as me. I don't mean to be different but if we are really going to become our own people I need to not treat you like my girlfriend, which I have been doing and it hurts too much,' she replied.

Oh God, I've lost her. She will never be mine again. We will never love each other again. No one is ever going to love me and I'm going to die alone.

Earl: OK, this is even getting too miserable for me.
Wanda: Thank God, one of us said it.
Me: You two aren't meant to agree!

SCREWED UP, SLIMMED DOWN

Wanda: You *will* be loved again.
Earl: OK, that's where we disagree.
Me: All I want to do is drive over to see Cat and hold her and kiss her and be so bloody close to her.
Earl: Christ, this is getting embarrassing.
Wanda: You can do this without her, my darling. You are loved and you will love again.
Me: I need to take a propranolol.

The day after she'd texted me telling me that she was pulling away I woke up and cried for two hours. I know that I ended the relationship and that I wanted her to have a life and become independent, but I didn't want to lose her as my person at the same time. But I can't have it both ways. She's going to find herself and I'm going to find myself and we will be fantastic friends in the future and it will be really good. I'm sure of it…

Wanda: Patience Jenna, it will come.
Me: I feel like I'm breaking all over again. Like this is the *actual* breakup and the first breakup was just a pretend one.
Wanda: Remember, Jenna, it wasn't working, you were both miserable and life would've gotten worse for both of you if you hadn't both agreed to go out and live. So let's start living!

From here on out I will stop looking to Cat to make me feel safe, wanted and worthy. I need to do this for myself! It's going to be lonely as hell, but I *will* do it. Until then, I will down five pints of beer in the pub tonight with some tennis friends and probably scoff a huge bowl of cereal when I get home.

But tomorrow, oh, tomorrow, it's a new day, bbz! I will make healthy choices, I will focus on my writing, on my work (eugh, snooze) and then I'm going to have fun at tennis and be the best Jenna that I can be.

SCREWED UP, SLIMMED DOWN

I *can* get over Cat and I *will* be OK on my own. One day I'll find my own Brandi Carlile (hot lesbian country singer) and until then I will embrace my new spinster status and find out who Jenna really is on her own. She might be really fucking fabulous, who knows?

CHAPTER 31

I AM NOW A MEDIUM

Cat came round last night for dinner and we had a lovely time. We chatted and it was all very pleasant, until…

'I had an interesting call with my mum the other day,' I said as we ate the banging meal I'd cooked (I had veggie sausages and she had meat ones because since we broke up she's gone back to eating meat). 'I was telling her about how sad I feel about our breakup and she asked how I'll feel when you start dating again.'

Cat put her knife and fork down and looked at me.

'Why did she ask that?'

'I've no idea. As if I want to feel any worse at the moment,' I laughed. I'm sure my mum didn't *mean* to make me feel horrendously more terrible… I looked up at Cat who wasn't saying anything. '*Have* you started dating yet?' I asked.

She paused. It was just a little pause, but it was a noticeable pause.

'No,' she said. 'Have you?'

'No, I'm not ready. We both said we'd not date anyone else for ages. You can't just end an eight-year relationship – well, it was a marriage really – and then immediately start dating.'

SCREWED UP, SLIMMED DOWN

Later on, as I walked into the living room with our desserts, I could see that Cat had tears in her eyes.

'What's wrong, love?'

'I lied,' she said.

'Oh, OK, what did you lie about?' I put the desserts on the table.

'I have been on a date, a few weeks ago.'

'Oh.'

Silence. My heart sank. She's been on a date, with someone else. We haven't even been separated for two months and a few weeks ago she went on a date. Fuck…

'I downloaded Tinder and I kept deleting it and I felt terrible but then I got chatting to someone and we met and I felt more terrible!'

'OK… And how did it go?' I mumbled, suddenly not wanting to eat dessert (which in itself is a travesty).

'It was fine. I probably won't see her again.' I didn't know how to respond so I just sat there and stared at my legs.

'She's not funnier than me, is she?' I asked eventually, trying to lighten the mood even though my mind suddenly felt like a tornado of thoughts and emotions.

'No,' Cat laughed.

Of course she isn't funnier than me… Please.

I cried, Cat cried, she said she felt like she'd done something wrong, like she was cheating on me. She said, a few minutes after saying that she probably *wasn't* going to see her again, that she *might* see her again.

She told me this woman's name, her job and that she has an 11-year-old daughter. I didn't want to know anything else, I told her to stop talking and I went into my bedroom, took off my wedding ring that I'd been wearing on my middle finger and put it in the drawer.

When she left my flat I had to get out and distract myself from all the thoughts in my head – after I'd gone on Facebook to see what this woman looked like of course, meh, dull. I drove to Sainsbury's, I needed to squash these feelings down with purchases. I didn't want to buy food (which is only the first time in all of my life that my anxiety has got so bad that I didn't want to binge it away with sugar).

Walking over to the clothes department, I picked up a grey zip-up hoodie in a Large. I tried it on and looked at myself in the mirror. My eyes were puffy and red like a baboon's arse.

No, surely I couldn't be a… no. It's not possible… Yes, I've lost two stone since the beginning of the year and my belly is now a few inches smaller, but this Large couldn't be… *too* big, could it?

I tried on the Medium, zipped it up and looked back up at the mirror. It fitted. For the first time in over nine years, I fit into a Medium. My ex of eight years has already been on a date within six weeks of us breaking up, but I'm a mother-trucking Medium. A single tear fell down my face.

Unfortunately, the buzz of me fitting into a medium-sized hoodie fizzled out as soon as I returned to my flat and got into bed.

'Hi, you alright?' Cat said as she answered the phone. Yes, I called her, I know it's not the right thing to do, but whatever, I needed answers.

'Hi, yeah, I was just wanting to ask a question about the whole date thing.'

'OK.'

'I just don't get it – if you loved me like you said you did, then how can you go on a date with someone less than two months after we broke up?'

'That hurts, Jenna. I wanted to marry you, even after everything we've been through I still wanted you, but then you broke up with me, so it really hurts that you think I didn't love you.'

'It just doesn't make sense to me,' I said.

'What do you want me to say, Jenna?' she said sternly. 'We don't know what's going to happen in the future, but I need to live my own life, because I haven't been, Jenna.

I've been waiting for you to change your mind and I'm not waiting anymore.'

We ended the call on OK terms, but the seed of despair had already been planted and the panic began to rise up. It was *huge* this time. Bigger than any attack I've ever had.

'I can't do this, I can't do this, oh God. I can't do this!' I cried to myself. I tried to soothe myself and take a propranolol but nothing was working. I wanted to scream, I wanted to cut myself, I wanted to die. Without being too dramatic, I wanted to *actually* die.

Jamie and Josie were on holiday so I had no one. I had no choice, I either walk into my bathroom and grab my razor to cut myself (I haven't done this in over 10 years) or I call Cat again.

I called her again, but she didn't answer. So much for always being there for me… But then two minutes later she called me back and she was lovely and I apologised for calling her, for having a panic attack, for everything. But I told her that I couldn't deal with it on my own, and I needed her to talk me down.

She talked me through the attack and tried to reassure me that everything was going to be OK.

'We've just got a new relationship now, another relationship may grow or we may just become friends, best friends and each other's confidantes, but right now, Jenna, we need to go through this sucky bit. But everything is OK. You are OK.'

Eventually, I managed to calm down and cry myself to sleep and when I woke up this morning I felt ashamed. I had been so full of despair and I had gone to the one person that I shouldn't go to. It was pathetic, I am at the very lowest point in my life.

Cat might have talked me down last night, but that is the *last* time I turn to her for help. I will *never* need anyone else to talk me down from a panic attack again. This I promise myself.

CHAPTER 32

AM I A SHIT SHAG?

I was cycling to tennis this evening when I started to laugh to myself.

'I can do those things on my own,' I said out loud as I waited for the red lights to change to green. 'I can do the North Coast 500, the New Zealand trip and the weekend in New York on my own.' I chuckled. Yes, it'll be tough and a wee bit lonely, but I can do it. I'm going to go out and live. And I can do it on my own! Well, goddamn, am I feeling empowered!

Solitude will help me find out who I am again. I've forgotten who I was before Cat, but now is the time to find myself again. Shall I do something drastic like shave my head? Get a neck tattoo? Become celibate? Well, the first two are a possibility and would come as no shock to my mother, but it's a hard no to the latter; orgasms are fun and I've rather missed them.

Can I sleep with another woman? What if she realises that I'm a bit shit? *Am* I a bit shit? No one has ever told me that…

SCREWED UP, SLIMMED DOWN

Wanda: No, Jenna, you're not shit and you will go out and shag again.

Gosh, that sounds so uncouth, I do apologise. I'm going to go travelling, I'm going to talk to people and I'm going to find other women to have fun sexy times with. God, I really hope my parents have stopped reading.

'That's fantastic, Jenna,' my therapist said to me today when I told her about my plans. 'You can absolutely do things on your own, sometimes things are better on your own.'

'Oh absolutely! I can now watch tennis on the TV in the evenings and not have to watch it on my iPad because Cat doesn't want to watch it.'

My therapist laughed to herself, probably because she's got a husband and a kid so I imagine she never gets to decide what's on the TV.

'So how are you feeling about Cat dating?' she asked.

'At the moment I'm trying not to think about it and instead focus on me. I realised that Cat and I were two halves of an apple and I don't want to be half an apple. I want to be a full apple and come together with another person who is also a full apple so that we can make a fruit bowl. So I'm working on myself to make sure that I become a full apple. I think Cat going on the dating scene so quickly is her way of not wanting to make herself a full apple. If that makes sense.'

'Yes, I understand what you mean,' she laughed. 'What you will find is that some days you'll feel like a big juicy apple and other days you'll feel like just the pip, but don't get discouraged by those pip days. Let's try and make you into the juiciest apple by the time you go on holiday with Cat.'

'I think my favourite apple-flavoured dessert is an apple crumble with ice cream,' I told her as I was leaving the session.

'Mine is an apple turnover,' she replied.

SCREWED UP, SLIMMED DOWN

'Hmm, good choice.'

Time to turn myself into a big fat apple.

CHAPTER 33

MY INNER CHILD NEEDS TO SHUT IT

September

Cat and I are off on our two-week American holiday tomorrow. We're going to Denver, New Orleans and then finishing off in Miami and it's, hopefully, going to be flipping epic. In preparation for what will be a very emotionally charged two weeks with my ex I had a last-minute therapy session earlier today.

'I've written a list of rules for the holiday,' I told my therapist as we started to discuss how I was feeling about the trip.

'That's great. What are they?'

'Number one: do not ask a single bloody thing about Cat's new girlfriend. Number two: do not ask if Cat still loves or misses me. Number three: do not get too drunk. And number four: no letting Cat pop any of the blackheads on my back.'

'Oh, is that something she does, then?'

'Yeah, throughout our entire relationship she liked to climb on my back like a spider monkey and pore over every inch of my skin in search for spots and blackheads. But no more, because that's what *girlfriends* do, not friends,' I said triumphantly.

'That's fantastic, Jenna. That sounds like you're adding boundaries and really working on the self-preservation stuff that we spoke about last week.' She smiled at me. 'Can I add some more rules to your list?'

'Sure.'

'Be kind to yourself and remember you're still healing. When you're out and about, look for the positives and treat yourself – if you normally get two scoops of ice cream, get three.' Please, I normally get 12.

Later on in the session we were joined by a third person: young Jenna, aka, my inner child. She's 14, she wears thick black makeup to match her clothes and mood, and she appears whenever I feel triggered. For some reason I've only just realised that she's been here all along.

Earl: I like your inner child, she's my favourite of the voices in your head.
Me: Of course she is, because you're basically her.

I explained to my therapist about how sometimes I get this flood of despair and primal rejection if someone does something that's different, or makes me feel left out.

'When I was at university, my friend always sent me her blog post to read before she published it. But one day she published it without sending it to me and I got this huge stab of rejection.'

'And what were the thoughts around this feeling?' she asked.

'That she didn't like me anymore, that I didn't matter anymore, that I'm left out and a piece of shit.'

We spoke more about what this meant and she explained that these type of events are triggering my inner child because I never dealt with those feelings at the time. When I was younger I felt isolated, lonely and rejected by certain friends and family members, and young Jenna didn't know how to deal with those feelings, so she ate herself silly to repress the feelings.

'So now, even though you're an adult, when something happens to make you feel a bit rejected, all these repressed, undealt-with feelings come back up. So, the thing that happened with your friend not sending you the blog post is a tiny pebble being dropped into a nice calm lake – but when the pebble reaches the water it turns into a huge boulder and that's why you're flooded by these overwhelming emotions,' she explained.

We explored the notion that I don't have to react that way to people's behaviour anymore. Young Jenna didn't know how to deal with these feelings, but adult Jenna does. She can try to rationalise someone's behaviour, she can get her self-worth internally and not externally – and she can see that it's not personal against her. Well, I'm *trying* to do these things. Baby steps.

'When someone doesn't text you back for hours, how do you feel?' she asked.

'Crushed to the very core. It tells me that clearly our friendship doesn't mean anything to that person, so our friendship is obviously over and I'm just a stupid desperate idiot who has been thrown out with the rubbish,' I replied without missing a beat.

'But could there be another reason why someone wouldn't reply straight away?'

'Probably…' I replied, rolling my eyes like a sulky teenager.

'And what could some of those reasons be?'

'They could be busy at work, they could be busy with something else, they might not be feeling very good so they don't have the mental energy to reply or, I guess, they might just want to reply when they've thought of a response or they have more time.'

'Exactly. Other people's actions aren't about you, they're not taking so long to reply because they hate

Jenna.'

This felt so important and poignant in my therapy journey. It makes *so* much sense that the next time something like that happens, sure, I might initially still react in the same way, but I will learn bit by bit that I don't need to react like that and it's not a reflection of my self-worth. Other people's actions *aren't* about me.

When I got home from therapy Cat and I had a video call to finalise stuff for the holiday and she told me that she and her new girlfriend, let's call her Bitch Face (I'm sure she's not a bitch face and she's an amazingly lovely woman, but for the sake of protecting her identity let's call her 'Bitch Face'), are now exclusively together.

'She's not like anyone I've ever dated,' Cat said.

'In what way?' I asked.

'She's a size eight.'

Oh wow… Could you imagine if I'd said that? If I'd said, 'Hey Cat, my new girlfriend is like no one I've ever dated, because *she's thin*.'

Who is this new Cat? I don't know her, but I'm off to America for two weeks with her, so fingers crossed she's not a total knob.

CHAPTER 34

AN ENGLISH MUFFIN IN DENVER

Day One: post-breakup American holibobs

I'm sitting in business class on my way to Denver, right now. I know, I'm a fancy bitch. But to be fair it was only £400 more than economy, so I thought, 'Bollocks, why not?'

I got to Heathrow early, checked in my bag and wandered around WH Smith looking at the books with pure excitement rushing through my veins. I bloody *love* travelling! Even if it is with my ex who has a new size-eight girlfriend.

Once I'd checked in I waited for Cat to arrive. My childish inner Jenna was like, 'Oh, I'm sure she's going to have a cigarette and call Bitch Face before she gets into the terminal, nerrrrr.'

As I waited for her to arrive, I browsed the luggage-wrapping device and, as I tilted my head to the side to read the instructions, someone came up behind me and kicked me on the bum. I turned around to see Cat with a huge smile on her face beaming up at me (she wasn't sat on the floor, she's just quite short). We hugged tightly. I've really missed hugging her.

We went through security and then made our way to

the business-class lounge where a free buffet of proper posh grub was waiting for us. When I say 'free', I mean 'food and drink that we've already paid for in the price of our flight ticket'. The buffet was full of quinoa, tiny ham hock pies and weird salads. There wasn't a chip or pizza slice to be found, and as for dessert – there was fruit. I'm sure you'll agree that fruit doesn't count as dessert, unless it's covered in chocolate or custard.

The mood between Cat and I is fine so far; there's an equal balance of warmth and awkwardness, which is to be expected. We were both smiling and playing about with each other as we boarded the plane and made our way to our seats – business bloody class, darling.

We have our own private little cubicle each with a tiny door, so I can't actually see her – though I did see her take a cute selfie just before we took off. Oh, I wonder who that's for…

I waited until we had been in the air for at least an hour before I started on the free Heinekens (again, paid for, not free, so I shouldn't feel bad when ordering two at a time) and I hope that once this *Star Wars* movie I'm watching is done I can get a couple of hours' sleep so that the jet lag isn't too much of a dick when we land in Denver.

I haven't signed up to the Wi-Fi because it's $5 (why the hell isn't *this* free?!). Cat has signed up to the Wi-Fi, of course she has – she's in that exciting part of her new relationship where you can't go five minutes without texting each other. Oh, look, here's a picture of me in business class, aww, you look so cute, have a safe flight, mwah mwah mwah. Puke.

Jamie has told me many times that Cat moving on with her love life is not anything personal, it's *her* stuff and it *isn't* a rejection of me. I am whole on my own. Now where the hell is that air steward with my next two Heinekens?

Day Two: post-breakup American holibobs
Why have we come to Denver? Well, my favourite country

singer and future wife Brandi Carlile is on tour and for some reason she's not coming to the local arts centre in Hove, so I've had to fly 4,683 miles to see her.

I've been looking forward to this concert so bloody much that I was worried that I might die before it happened. Isn't that right, Earl?

> **Earl:** Certainly is. It's best not to look forward to things, because you might die before they happen.
> **Me:** This isn't the first time you've told me this though, is it?
> **Earl:** Nope.
> **Me:** What else have you done this with?
> **Earl:** The last season of *Game of Thrones*.
> **Me:** That's right. I was *so* looking forward to seeing what would happen to Daenerys and her big fiery dragons that I got a bit existential about not surviving long enough to see it.
> **Earl:** And then when you *did* survive long enough to see it, it was a total disappointment.
> **Me:** Yes, it was.
> **Earl:** And why was that?
> **Me:** Because life is one big disappointment?
> **Earl:** I have taught you well, young Padawan.

The show tonight was at the Red Rocks Amphitheatre in Denver, an open-air amphitheatre built into a rock structure that is incredibly beautiful and incredibly bloody cold – because, you know, it's outside in the middle of a bunch of rocks… Unfortunately, two seconds after we arrived at the concert the heavens opened and me, ever the ninny brain, was only wearing a shirt and a pair of jeans, so it was fecking freezing.

In order to warm up I had to drink a few beers (well, one does what one can to survive). So before the show started I was cold, wet and drunk. And then Brandi came on stage and it was the best night of my life.

The show was epic and everything I imagined it would be. I was the full unfiltered Jenna for the *entire* show, singing my heart out, doing all the dancing and living in the pure joy of the moment.

During the show she sang 'The Story', which is the song that Cat and I were supposed to walk down the aisle to at our wedding – and when the first few notes began to play, I burst into tears.

I put my arm around Cat, pulled her close and kissed her head as the tears streamed down both of our faces. We had our arms around each other, both singing the lyrics aloud for the entire song. It was an incredibly special moment.

Day Three: post-breakup American holibobs

Today I woke up with an epic hangover, as expected. I have anxiety, beer fear, and all the emotions to do with Cat, life and death – so I think I'll give alcohol a rest for a good few days.

Cat has been texting and calling Bitch Face quite a bit, though she does do it away from me (aka when she goes outside for a fag), which is thoughtful, though it does still suck. She's moved on. She doesn't need me and she's got her new exciting life and relationship without me. My inner child has been triggered, hard.

Cat was away for 45 minutes this morning for her fag, I thought she might have been kidnapped or something. What has happened between last night's phone call to this morning's one that causes her to talk for 45 minutes? I mean, who has that much to say?!

Today I am going to try and ignore all of the texts and calls, and every time she *does* text and call Bitch Face I'm going to meditate for 10 seconds, and focus on my body. I will *not* crumble like an apple crumble with ice cream. I will be strong, like bull.

Day Three: post-breakup American holibobs cont'd

SCREWED UP, SLIMMED DOWN

OK, so I may have crumbled a wee bit… We were sat in a sports bar earlier watching the women's US Open tennis final and eating lunch. Cat was sat texting Bitch Face and I tried to ignore it but she was texting *a lot*. She then put her phone on the table face up in between us and a message popped up from 'English Muffin'.

'What does that say?' I asked in confusion, hoping that I'd completely misread it. Cat smiled and picked up her phone before swiping the message away and then placing the phone back down on the table, screen first.

'English Muffin,' she muttered, smirking to herself. 'I meant to change it.'

Heat immediately rose to my face. I felt sick. 'English Muffin', are you fucking kidding me? Her smile as she'd said it made it worse. I didn't know what to do in that moment. I wanted to throw the table against the wall and scream my head off (anger issues, me? No, I absolutely will not have it).

'I just need to get some air for a minute,' I mumbled, excusing myself from the table before my volcano of emotions exploded all over our food.

I left the restaurant and paced up and down Denver high street swearing my head off along with all the drunks and homeless people swearing *their* heads off. At least my swearing was somewhat coherent.

Warning sensitive readers, sweary bit coming up:

'How the fuck are you there with someone already? Cute fucking pet names? Are you *fucking* kidding me? English Muffin? How the hell did you ever love me? Did you leave your phone turned up so I'd see it?! Of course you did, fucking hell!'

I've never had so much anger for someone than I did for Cat in that moment. The anxiety, sickness and anger wasn't just flooding my body, it *was* my body.

I felt like the biggest, saddest piece of shit who isn't over her ex and whose ex is totally over her and living her best life and just wants to text and call her new girlfriend, while I'm sat there like a stupid bloody plum.

When I returned to the restaurant I told Cat how it made me feel (as calmly as possible, of course). I told her that I didn't want to make her feel bad, but what had just happened made me feel utterly worthless.

She cried and said that she felt really bad and that the last thing she wanted to do was hurt me.

Cat texting and being all lovey-dovey with her new girlfriend in front of me reminded me of that time when I was 17 and having a sleepover with Hannah and our mutual male friend (Hannah being the friend I had unrequited love for at school, do keep up). Hannah and our friend knew exactly how I felt about her at that time, but they didn't give a damn about my feelings when they were busy canoodling and heavy petting in the bed next to me.

Seventeen-year-old Jenna cried silently in the bed, her heart breaking and her soul crumbling in despair and pain. And in that sports bar in Denver I was taken *straight* back to that feeling. Still, just 12 more days to get through and then I'll be back home with my tennis and my guinea pigs.

Just 12… More… Days…

Day Four: post-breakup American holibobs
Today has been much better. We went on a tour around the Rocky Mountains and it was breathtakingly beautiful. It was just like Scotland, only warmer and with fewer Scottish people.

When the tour guide arrived with his minivan we queued up to get in and he said that someone would have to ride shotgun in the front.

'Yeah, I will!' I said quickly before anyone else got the chance. If Cat and I had still been a couple, I wouldn't have volunteered to ride shotgun, because there was only one seat and I wouldn't have wanted her to feel left out. Plus, she would've been mad because as a codependent couple joined at the hip, we must sit together at all times. But now that I'm a singleton, I gave myself permission to put *myself* first – I enjoyed the scenic drive up to the mountains in the front and *she* sat in the back on her own – though I did swap with her halfway through because I'm not a total monster.

We had a few little stops on the tour and one of them was at 10,000 feet around Echo Lake, which was absolutely stunning, however, Cat was suffering from the altitude. Her breathing was shallow, her chest was tight and her heart rate was 148 at just a leisurely walking pace. I felt the altitude a bit in my head, but the worst thing was the bloating in my stomach – it was what I imagine being pregnant is like. I needed to let off the biggest fart ever, but I just couldn't push it out.

Cat also felt bloated, so when we came across a fence we both leaned on it and tried our best to push out our farts. I rubbed Cat's lower back to help her and she managed to sneak a little one out. Me, nothing; my bum hole had sewn itself up.

It was during this time that I knew that, no matter how much anger I had towards Cat, I still love her like family. You know, family – you detest them at times but if they need to fart, you'll happily lean over a fence and try and help them push one out.

Day Four: post-breakup American holibobs cont'd
Tonight we stood outside an ice cream parlour looking up at the flavours when I turned to Cat and said, 'Guess which one I'd pick.' This was a game we used to play all of the time when we were together, and she always got it right.

'It's out of the chocolate fudge brownie and the chocolate hazelnut,' she said, staring up at the menu on the wall. 'I'm going to say… chocolate fudge brownie!' She beamed with pride.

Now, I know that I see meaning in everything, but…

'No, I would've picked chocolate hazelnut because it's like Nutella,' I said sadly.

'Oh yeah…' she said, then turned back to her phone.

Oh yeah… Our unbreakable deep connection is slowly breaking.

Day Five: post-breakup American holibobs

This morning I was just about to get into the shower when I realised my razor was still in my suitcase, so I popped my towel on and went into our room to get the razor. Cat saw a blackhead on my back as I walked past her and she wanted to get it.

'Oh please, let me just get it. It's huge!' she cried.

'No, Cat.'

'Please, go on…' she said, following me back into the bathroom playfully.

I dropped my towel on the floor and stepped into the shower with her still in the room. That got her out quick! If we're just friends then you're not allowed to squeeze my blackheads… thems the rules, Cat, now why don't you go and call Bitch Face because you haven't called her for at least 30 minutes. Seriously, all these calls… You would've thought that she was a missing person.

CHAPTER 35

ANOTHER HUMAN BEING LIKES ME

Day Six: post-breakup American holibobs
After spending three days in what was, and I don't mean
to be judgemental here, the most boring shitting city in
America, we were super-excited when we arrived in jazz
party land, New Orleans, yesterday.

When we arrived at our hotel in the evening we quickly
unpacked and got ready to go out and explore the bars.
While Cat was on the toilet I asked if I could borrow her
lip balm. Sure, we don't share kisses anymore, but surely
we can share lip balm?

'Yeah, it's in the front of my little suitcase,' she replied.

I went into the front of her little suitcase to grab the lip
balm, but I couldn't find it. I had a good old rummage, but
still no lip balm. I then began to pull out all of the items
from the front pocket and put them on the floor: a face
mask, a lighter, a packet of chewing gum, a love note from
Cat's new girlfriend – oh, hold the bloody phone. What
the hell is this?

It was a postcard from Bitch Face to Cat that featured
big pink letters on the front that read 'You amazing thing,
you' and a handwritten love note on the other side. A huge
ball of dread and anxiety smacked me right in the face – I

could feel the anger rising. Just breathe, Jenna, just breathe. I tried to keep my cool, but the one thing I am *not* when I feel hurt is cool.

'HOW THE FUCK ARE YOU THERE WITH HER ALREADY?' I yelled, throwing the lip balm that I had eventually found hard against the wall.

'What? I can't hear what you're saying,' Cat said from the bathroom over the noise of the extremely loud air vent system.

'Nothing, I'm just talking to myself,' I said, trying to appear calm. 'How the hell are you there already? What did I mean to you? Oh, nothing, clearly, because you're already doing love notes with your new girlfriend!' I said to myself. I tried my best to focus on my breathing, focus on unpacking my own suitcase, just focus on anything that wasn't the love postcard that I'd angrily shoved back into her suitcase. But nothing was going to calm me down.

When Cat emerged from the bathroom she asked what I had said.

'Nothing, I'm just talking to myself. Sorry, I'm trying to keep it in, but I'm struggling.'

'Well, if you want to talk, we can. It's important to get things out.'

'I just don't get how you're there with her already!' I exploded.

'What the hell?' She looked genuinely shocked.

'How are you there with her already, with love notes, with calling and texting all the time? We've only been broken up for just over two months and suddenly you're absolutely fine and totally moved on with someone else.'

'Jenna, I didn't ask her to write that postcard, she just put it in my suitcase. Yeah, we're full on because I *am* full on, but I wasn't with you because you *weren't*. Do I love her? No. Am I having fun? Yes.'

'It just seems to me that you're fine and totally over me.'

'Jenna, I'm not, I have been crying and hurting and

SCREWED UP, SLIMMED DOWN

aching and waiting for you to change your mind and it got to a point where I just couldn't anymore. This thing with her is a distraction. Is she the love of my life? Are we getting married? No. But I'm trying to be fine because one of us has to be. We can't both fall apart.'

Me? Fall apart? OK, yeah, fair enough... Cat is, or at least *was*, the one person who knows me the most in this world and she is absolutely right – I have slowly begun to fall apart and if we both fall apart, then... well... I'm not sure what would happen, but it wouldn't be conducive to us enjoying our post-breakup American holibobs.

After we rehashed everything that had happened between us over the past year and the argument eventually died down, we went out to explore New Orleans' vibrant nightlife. It was just as wild as the nightlife we'd experienced in Bangkok a few years ago, only with fewer people shooting ping pongs out of their foofs.

The New Orleans streets were lined with jazz bars, tourist shops selling more tat than I could ever wish to buy and quirky (read: creepy and unhinged) voodoo ladies sitting on the street with a selection of tarot cards and candles in front of them, ready to tell me that my fortune is seriously about to come in.

As we walked down the street gawking at the scenes around us, a scantily clad woman holding a tray of laboratory test tubes filled with colourful alcohol shots approached Cat and barked at her to, 'Take a shot, take a shot!'

'What? What?' Cat said, smiling and giving the woman the unspoken green light.

The woman took two green test tubes from the tray, put the bottom of the test tubes in her own mouth and then bent over Cat and stuck the top of the test tubes into her mouth, tipping the alcohol in. It was like a mumma bird feeding a worm to a baby bird, but the mumma bird was a stranger, the baby bird was Cat and the worm was two test tubes full of apple Aftershock that we hoped

SCREWED UP, SLIMMED DOWN

hadn't been spiked.

The liquid went into Cat's mouth and the woman then started to thrust the tubes aggressively into Cat's mouth in a blow-job motion. I watched with shock and utter confusion.

'That's $30, baby,' the nearly naked woman said afterwards as she deposited the used test tubes back into the tray, looking bored by the whole thing.

'What? Cat, $30, what? Are you OK? What just happened?' I shrieked. But Cat ignored me and paid the money.

'Just keep walking; she might attack us if I don't pay,' she whispered, wiping the small bit of blood away from her mouth where one of the test tubes had cut her.

The woman looked over to me and then started to approach me with her tray of test tubes, but I ran away shouting, 'No, leave me alone! Leave me alone!'

Cat says 'yes' to life and I've always loved that about her, and I'm trying to be more like that, but that 'yes' was a hard bloody 'no' from me. Cat basically got face-raped and paid $30 for the privilege.

We ended the night in a gay karaoke bar, where we drank and watched other people wail as we waited for Cat's turn to sing.

'"Hopelessly Devoted to You", by Scottish Cat!' yelled the drag queen who was hosting the evening.

Cat got up on stage and sung the song while staring directly at me.

'*But now there's no way to hide, since you pushed my love aside. I'm hopelessly devoted to you.*' Every lyric had meaning, every line was about us, every single bloody thing in that song stabbed me in the heart, causing fresh pain.

There I was, sitting in a sticky gay bar in New Orleans watching my favourite person on earth (who was slowly slipping away from me) singing about it in front of the gayest homosexuals you've ever seen.

'After the holiday we need to take a break from each

other. We need to heal and digest and get over each other,' we agreed when we got back to the hotel.

We will be fine, I will be fine. When I'm back home and no longer having waffles with chocolate chips and ice cream for breakfast (God bless those Americans!) I will get back to my fitness, back to my healthy eating and back to being my bestest self for the rest of the year. As for now, I will cry myself to sleep while Cat lies on the other side of the bed texting Bitch Face goodnight. God, this nightmare is worse than that time I dreamt that my feet got eaten by guinea pigs.

Day Seven: post-breakup American holibobs

As we explored New Orleans today we walked along the Mississippi River, where we came across a fence full to the brim with padlocks with love hearts and couples' initials on. Yeah, well, I bet at LEAST 90 per cent of those people aren't together anymore.

Cat wanted us do the padlock thing in Paris after we'd only been together for a few months and it felt like it was too soon to commit to such a thing because, for me, it had a lot of meaning.

However, we did end up buying a padlock, putting our initials on it and then locking it to the bridge – it was lovely and I still have the key. I guess looking back now it really was a great example of how she's quite full on and I'm not. My thinking behind not wanting to do it was, 'I never want to get too close to someone or I might get hurt.' And here I was eight years later, hurt to the bloody bone.

Day Eight: post-breakup American holibobs

Thankfully, we've been getting on fantastically since the huge blowout on the first night.

'Let's go to the casino,' I suggested as we walked past a huge shiny Harrah's casino on the way back from eating beignets (little French doughnuts) in Cafe du Monde

SCREWED UP, SLIMMED DOWN

(overpriced tourist cafe). Louise had taken me to the casino back in Brighton a few times in the past few months, so I wanted to show off my newfound knowledge of the casino to Cat.

'Sure!'

We went into the most humongous casino that I've ever seen outside of Las Vegas and I immediately strode up to one of the many roulette tables.

'I can't remember how these work,' Cat said as she sat down on the stool and got her wallet out.

'Don't worry,' I nudged her as I sat down. 'I've done this a few times before,' I said, handing over my $15 to the bored-looking dealer who gave me a small pile of green chips in return. Cat handed over a $20 bill and got a pile of pink chips.

I placed five of my chips on various numbers on the table, sat back and smiled. Cat did the same.

'$15 minimum bet,' the dealer said, pointing to the sign that read '$15 minimum bet'.

'What? $15 minimum for every spin?' I shrieked. The dealer pointed to the sign again without making any eye contact with us. Clearly we were just stupid tourists who were wasting his time.

We placed all $35 worth of green and pink chips on the table (in the corners of the numbers to increase our chances of winning). By the time we had placed all of our chips on the table, there were only a couple of numbers that were not covered – our odds, in my newly expert opinion, were high.

The dealer span the roulette wheel, his face drooping further into boredom. The ball raced around the roulette wheel, bouncing and crashing around before finally landing on a number.

'Four,' the dealer mumbled.

Ah, number four – one of the only numbers that we didn't have covered…

'Let's wave goodbye to our money,' I said, waving at

SCREWED UP, SLIMMED DOWN

the chips as the dealer wiped them all off the table.

'Bye,' Cat said.

'Shall we leave?'

'Yeah.'

Day Nine: post-breakup American holibobs

I wouldn't say that New Orleans is hot, but my skin has melted and my blood has evaporated. Hence why I've been spending most of today by the hotel pool. I've left Cat in the hotel room and come down here on my own to, a) do some writing and, b) give Cat some space so that she can call Bitch Face without worrying that I'll suddenly appear.

When we were at the pool cooling off yesterday after our big casino loss, there was a man standing in the water sunning his face. Now, the hotel pool is quite small, so when Cat and I joined him in the pool it was oh so awkward. Obviously I wasn't going to do more than offer a polite grin – I'm from southern England, dammit, if this American bloke wants to chat then I'm afraid he's going to have to make the first move.

'Have you ladies just arrived?' the man asked in a very monotone southern English accent. Ah, one of my people… Marvellous.

We got talking to this man, Dean, and we had a lovely conversation about the brewery that he runs back in England. We also spoke about football (women's football, not the pretend crap that men play), travel, where we've been in America and our general uninformed opinions on the Biden administration.

'I'm a writer and comedian,' I told him sheepishly when he asked what I do for work.

'That's great, what sort of things do you write? Do you have a website?' he asked, showing genuine interest.

'I write humorous essays and sketches about lesbian culture and mental health.'

'That sounds great, how would I find your stuff

online?' he asked. I told him where he could find my work and then thought no more about it.

Back to this morning. Cat eventually came down to join me and we had the pool to ourselves for a while. I spent most of the time sat on a lounger writing on my iPad and Cat spent the time going between her lounger and the smoking area. Cat had just left the pool area to go for her second cigarette of the hour when Dean walked around the corner with his towel and book. I only saw him out of my peripheral vision, and even though we had such a lovely chat yesterday I did the southern English thing of totally ignoring him and pretending that I hadn't seen him.

'Hi, Jenna!' he called out.

'Hey, how you doing?' I said, sitting up on my lounger, giving my best 'oh I didn't see you there' expression. 'Don't worry, Cat will be back in a minute. She's just having a cigarette, so you don't have to talk to me for very long,' I didn't say, but very much thought.

'So, how's your writing going? Are you working on anything particular at the moment?' he asked, plopping himself in the pool.

What? This man was talking to *me*? But Cat was walking back to the pool now, so he only had to wait for a few seconds and then he could do all the chatting with her. She's Scottish for God's sake, talk to her! But no, here was a man who not only said hello to me, but also remembered my name *and* my occupation that I'd muttered stupidly at him. See, inner child/young Jenna, some people *do* like us and don't think we're a total annoying bore to be avoided. #win!

Throughout our entire relationship people normally just spoke to Cat because I've got a resting bitch face and she's the chatty one – she used to just talk for both of us.

Cat eventually joined us by the pool but then a few minutes later she went back up to the hotel room while Dean and I continued to talk. I don't know what came over me but I felt safe to tell him exactly what was going

SCREWED UP, SLIMMED DOWN

on.

'Me and Cat are actually ex-girlfriends,' I told him, 'we'd booked this holiday before we broke up, so we're trying to have the best time possible. But she's got a new girlfriend now so it's been pretty difficult.'

'That sounds really tough. Well, you look like you're doing really well, so good for you.'

Later that evening (after he'd clearly stalked my Facebook and found my online comedy sketches about my recent weight-loss journey) he sent me a message:

'Hi Jenna, great to meet you and Cat. You're also looking great with the weight loss, even though you're in the food excess country of the world right now. Hope you find what you're looking for next and good luck with your writing career. If it helps, I'd never run a business before setting up my brewery seven years ago and I haven't looked back. Go for your dreams or you'll regret it.'

During a time when I thought that no one would ever be interested in me as a human being again, this genuinely lovely man and I made a connection. I may even message him back – God, how bloody forward of me.

CHAPTER 36

GOODBYE TO THE OLD JENNA

Day 12: post-breakup American holibobs
I'm sitting in the lobby of our Miami hotel on the last leg of our post-breakup American holibobs. We've been in Florida for a few days already and the one word I can use to describe Miami is 'hot'. Like, so hot that even the beasty thunder, biblical downpours and almighty cracks of lightning haven't been able to lower the temperature.

Cat woke me up today at 8:15 am to tell me that she was going for a fag. I didn't need to be awoken to learn this information, she could have just gone for a fag, but no, she decided to wake me up and tell me before buggering off for 30 minutes.

I know you're off to speak to your girlfriend, Cat, you don't need to wake me up early to tell me.

That pissed me off, so when she returned to the room I was blasting 'Good 4 u' by Olivia Rodrigo, singing the following lyrics with extra oomph:

'*Well, good for you, I guess you moved on really easily. You found a new girl, and it only took a couple of weeks.*'

I hope that she got the message. I plan to use this song as my alarm clock for the next two days as well – just to really hammer the point home.

As we were sat sunbathing after lunch today, Cat told me that she wasn't in love with me anymore.

'I still love and care about you, but I'm not in love with you anymore.'

Wow, it's always great to hear that; please, could you say it again but louder this time so that everyone around the pool can hear?

Day 13: post-breakup American holibobs

We've only got one day left of this big emotional holibobs, and like the sensitive little lesbian I am, I've written Cat a letter to give to her when we land back at Heathrow.

My darling Cat,

Thank you for the most amazing and memorable holiday. This trip to America was always going to be awesome and hard in equal measure and it didn't disappoint. That night at Red Rocks seeing Brandi Carlile will stay with me forever, it was truly one of the best nights of my life.

That moment when I kissed your head and pulled you in close when she sang 'The Story' (our should've been wedding song) and we sung and swayed together was really special and I will treasure that memory always.

We both know that we have to have a clean break from each other to heal and get over what we've been through these past few years. But I want you to know that I will always love you. You are and will always be one of the biggest loves of my life.

I want more than anything for you to be happy and I know that I haven't been able to deal with you moving on as well as I'd hoped, but I don't want you to feel guilty or bad or like a big hairy arsehole, because you're not and you shouldn't ever feel guilty for putting your happiness first. For the past few years you've put my happiness before your own, which wasn't the right thing for either of us, so now you have the chance to do a new relationship make sure you put YOU first.

And don't be too lesbian, OK, just chill and take things at a good pace because I can see you getting married and having kids in

SCREWED UP, SLIMMED DOWN

like a month or two and even in lesbo-land that's too quick. Codependency was a big issue in our relationship and I'd hate for either of us to fall back into that trap.

Our relationship is no longer going to be one where we bang each other, but I really hope that we can get to a place where we are best friends and super-close again because to me you are and will always be my darling. My family.

You have brought me so much joy in the eight years we spent together. You've helped me grow and you've been there to save me in the darkest of moments. Now it's time for me to do that for myself.

I will always look back on our travels and life with a huge amount of love and happiness. From your face when I first brought the guinea pigs home, to your face when you were shitting and puking on the toilet in Thailand. The bestest memories.

Anyway, now it's time to not be so soppy because I'm currently writing this in the lobby of our Miami hotel and I'm crying and the silly Americans in suits who have just come out of a finance conference are staring at me.

I love you, Cat, and I can't wait to see what the future brings for both of us separately, but together.

I love you millions and always.
Poopy Face

(Jenna, your hilarious ex-girlfriend with the fuzzy butt / the one who got away)

I then wrote myself a letter, because I really *am* that much of a sensitive little lesbian.

Dear Me,

We're currently sat in the lobby of a Miami hotel crying after having written our ex-girlfriend a letter that we plan to give her when we land back in the UK. It's the most lesbian emotional letter ever written, because my dear, you / I am a precious little poppet with lots of feelings.

You've just spent the best and worst two weeks of your life with

SCREWED UP, SLIMMED DOWN

your ex-girlfriend travelling across America. You've eaten, drunk and consumed your yearly recommended allowance of food, alcohol and feelings, and it's time to put your big-girl pants on and sort your shit out.

Now, when we get home we're going to lose the half a stone you've put on in America (half a stone, yah suuuuuure, let's say it's more like a full stone, darling). We're going to have a break from the ex-girlfriend. If you want to be friends with her in the future then we must take time to heal.

We will see her at our friend's wedding in December and, baby, we are going to look HOT. I mean so ridiculously hot, we're going to be physically at PEAK JENNA and mentally, oh goddamn, we're going to have our shit sorted out.

Don't worry your pretty little head about the crap we ate and felt on holiday, we had the best time and those 12 waffles and six double cheeseburgers and endless arguments won't matter one little bit in a few weeks.

It's now time for 'new Jenna' and she's going to be the absolute making of us.

All my love and farts,
Jenna

CHAPTER 37

THE NEW JENNA HAS ARRIVED

October

Hello and welcome to the new Jenna, she's absolutely fabulous and she's got her shit sorted out. OK, she hasn't *quite* got her shit sorted out, but she's a real work in progress, darling.

When I got back from America I was elated, I was so happy, I was free from the pain of my breakup, free from the sight of Cat texting and calling her new girlfriend and I was back in my flat. My lovely flat with my two lovely guinea pigs (me referring to them as 'lovely' will be short-lived), my lovely tennis friends, my lovely non-tennis friends and most importantly, my freedom.

While I was in America I partook in the consumption of cheeseburgers, waffles, Philly cheesesteaks, waffles, beasty sandwiches, cheesecakes, waffles, fries and waffles. OK, it was a *lot* of waffles.

On the last day of the holibobs we took my International House of Pancakes virginity by stopping off at one of their restaurants on the way to the airport – it was filthy, messy and disgustingly beautiful. French toast with syrup and cream for breakfast? Holy Jesus and his little donkey, it was heaven. To be honest, I'm actually

SCREWED UP, SLIMMED DOWN

surprised that Americans aren't *fatter*.

Before the holiday I was 13 stone 8 pounds and when I stepped on the scales the day after I arrived back home, I looked down and saw… oh crap… 13 stone 10 pounds. What? Who? How? Two pounds? That's it?? Hell yeah!!

Two mother-trucking pounds! Incredible… I was expecting to put on *at least* half a stone (and that was going to be a good outcome).

But, if I look back at my time on holiday I actually did do a lot of cycling, a lot of walking, some scooting about *and* I sweated and cried out a lot of water retention, so really, if you think about it, I'm surprised I didn't *lose* weight. This is an excellent start to the new exciting Jenna for the last quarter of the year!

Tonight, I went around my flat putting everything that reminded me of Cat into a box. Every letter, every picture, every piece of admin from our life together – I don't want to accidentally see any of it.

I've taken down the paint-by-numbers picture of Baby Yoda that she did for me and I've replaced it with a picture of my favourite emo band, My Chemical Romance, from my teenage years. As I gently folded the Baby Yoda painting I saw on the back that Cat had written 'Love always, Cat '22'.

'Oh, look at that, Mummy loves other Mumma "always" apparently…' I said to Rusty and Tiny Tim who were impatiently waiting to be fed.

It's been a couple of days since I got back from America and during the first couple of days I tried my best to stay friends with Cat on Facebook without giving into the temptation to look at her profile.

Earl: Have a look at Cat and her new girlfriend's profile picture. Let the anxiety poison your mind. Do it! Do it now!!

Wanda: Take control of your happiness, Jenna, remove her from your Facebook and focus on YOU!

I did it, I took Cat off my Facebook and I blocked her and Bitch Face (who I will no longer be referring to as Bitch Face because, actually, I'm growing as a person and also I don't care enough about this woman to give her such a funny name. From now on I'll be referring to her as FKA Bitch Face).

Yes, I had anxiety when I actually did the ceremonious blocking of Cat, but I need to stop worrying about being nice and pleasing everyone and just do what is best for *me*. At the moment, not having the option of looking at Cat's social media and seeing pictures of her seemingly happy new life is what is best for me.

So far this year I've lost two and a half stone and my goal for these last few months is to lose another stone.

To do this I'm going to continue with the intermittent fasting, continue with 'Jenna's form of keto' and also start incorporating weights into my exercise routine, aka, actually start lifting the dumbbells that I bought with good intentions and not just use them as doorstops.

My friends Jamie and Josie are getting married in mid-December and it's currently the beginning of October. Cat and I have agreed to go no contact until the wedding, so I've got just over two months to get as fit, sexy and mentally tiptop as possible. Not because I want her back, but because there's no better revenge than a life well lived. (Not that I want revenge on her, but still, it'll inflate my delicate ego if I'm able to be the best version of myself the next time I meet my past.)

And that's what Cat represents for me now, my past. One day we might be friends and she'll represent my present, but not today – she's my past and my past doesn't need me. My future does.

Wanda: Yeah it does!!

At the beginning of the year I was having regular panic

attacks that crippled me mentally, but I haven't had a single attack since the night that I found out Cat was dating someone new and that was over a month ago. Was it my doubts about the relationship that was causing my panic attacks? Was it living in Haywards Heath and not seeing a way out? Or was it because I'd made my life so small that everything seemed scary and overwhelming? Perhaps a combination of all three…

I'm so excited for this new, happy, sexy Jenna; soon she's going to be under 13 stone, she's going to be happy and panic-attack free and she's going to smash the rest of this year with her big-girl pants on.

> **Wanda:** And maybe she'll end up having lots of fun sex with someone! Woo hoo orgasms!
> **Me:** No, Wanda, I'm focusing on me, not my vagina.
> **Wanda:** Your vagina is still part of you.
> **Me:** Hmm, you make a very good point…

CHAPTER 38

LUCKY NUMBER FOUR

'No more bets, please,' called the dealer as Louise and I finished placing our chips on the roulette table in Brighton. 'Twenty-seven,' he said, sweeping away everyone's chips. This was the first time back at a casino since that bad time in New Orleans.

It wasn't long until I was down to my last chip. Number five is my lucky number and I was born on the 29th, so I would normally go for both of those, but with one chip left, which one would get it? My lucky number, or the date I came into existence…

'I'll go for a straight four,' I said, placing my last chip in the middle of number four.

'No more bets, please,' the dealer said as the ball in the roulette wheel slowed down. The ball bounced around the wheel, bouncy, bouncy, bouncy, and as the wheel slowed even more the ball landed in its final place.

'Number four,' the dealer said, popping the marker on top of my chip and sweeping away all the losing chips.

'Number four! I won!' I shrieked at Louise, in a totally cool and not at all embarrassing way. That's a £1 chip bet on 35 to 1, which (Louise told me) meant I'd just won £35, on the *same number* that Cat and I had lost $35 on.

SCREWED UP, SLIMMED DOWN

Now, I believe in all the fate/divine/kombucha energy as much as the next person, but this was something else. This was the Universe giving me a big bollocking sign.

Yes, it's only £35, but the meaning behind it... oh, such meaning... Number four with Cat in America lost us dollar, but number four with my new friend in my new life brought me the win. Oh, Universe, you cheeky thing.

'Right, let's go before I gamble this £35 away,' I said excitedly, getting up from the table to leave the big boys to it. And when I say 'big boys', I mean middle-aged men in jogging bottoms holding huge wads of cash betting on multiple tables at once. Compare them to me with my little win and you may say that I was the loser there, but actually, I was happier than a dog with two tails (which is *such* an odd phrase).

CHAPTER 39

I QUIT MY JOB, SHIT...

I quit my job yesterday. Do I have a new job to go to? No. Do I plan to get a new job? No. Have I just won big at the casino? No... (£35 doesn't even *begin* to cover my avocado bill for the month – damn you, keto!). But am I going to stop wasting my life on my B plan and start trying to live my dream, aka the A plan? Yes!

I'm going to try and make it as a writer. To make it as a writer means that I actually need to have the time to write, and at the moment I don't even have time to pick my nose, because after finishing my day job I'm mentally too twatted to do anything other than just sit there and stare at the wall.

I wrote my resignation letter the other day while I was working from home and thinking, 'Nah, I don't want to do this anymore.' If I get an illness next week I will obviously be devastated, but I'll also be incredibly frustrated that I didn't try to make something of my life while I still had the chance.

I know that sounds like a really negative way of looking at life, but actually, it's just a mix of Earl and Wanda.

Earl: You might get a terminal illness next week.

SCREWED UP, SLIMMED DOWN

Wanda: Then it's time to do something with your life!
Me: Seriously, are you two psychos forming an allegiance?

Once I'd written my resignation letter I said to myself that I wouldn't send it right away, instead I'd wait until the next day to see if I still felt the same way. Lo and behold, what do you know – I felt exactly the same.

I've wanted to quit my job and write for *years*, but I've never done it because I've always been too scared to take the jump. Also, if I had quit my job while I was still with Cat and things had gone financially wrong then it wouldn't have just been me who suffered. But now that it's just me and my fluffy guinea pig children (who are, unfortunately for them, getting lots of cuddles every night to help me from the crippling loneliness), I'm a lot freer to make these wild decisions regarding my own happiness.

Me quitting my job wasn't a big impulsive decision and nor was it a decision that I overthought within an inch of its life. Because that's been my problem whenever I've needed to make a decision in my life, I overthink it so much that I end up frozen in fear because there's no *right* answer to anything.

Allow me to give you an example:

Should I buy this new pen? Well, I like this pen and I will use it, but also I don't *need* another pen, plus it's made of non-recyclable plastic so when it inevitably runs out I'll have to throw it away, which is bad for the planet. But I want it and it'll make me happy for a few moments and we've only got one life so I should just buy it, but what about the planet? And is it worth the money? Is this where my hoarding disorder begins? And that's *just* a pen – no wonder it's taken me so long to start taking action on the bigger things.

'I'm handing in my resignation today,' I told my boss after taking her into a room so that we could have some privacy.

'Oh no, Jenna... Oh God, I'm so sorry to hear that. Is there anything we can do to make you stay?' she asked, genuinely gutted at the idea of me leaving.

'No, I'm going to write for a few months. It's my dream to be a writer and I've got a little following online so I feel it's the best time for me to really go for it,' I said, trying my best not to sound like an absolute wanker.

'I'm really gutted, Jenna. But you're right, if you want to be a writer then you have to go and do it. It's great that you've got a following, how many followers have you got? My friend has about half a million on Instagram, I think.'

OK, so when I said I've got a little bit of a following online, I meant just that, a *little* bit. Since the beginning of the year I've been uploading a video every week documenting my progress on my weight loss and my mental health journey, which has caused my online following to grow in popularity. I'm not quite at Justin Bieber level yet though...

'I've got about 6,000 followers on Facebook...' I told her, feeling like the biggest idiot ever – like when the marketing girl gets 12 likes on her first TikTok video and she quits her job to make it in the big time. 'It's only small, but it's enough to build my platform on and write my book.'

'Oh great, what's the book about?'

'It's about me losing weight and sorting out my mental health,' I told her, which I'm sure she found somewhat amusing considering it was only six weeks ago that I was running to the toilet to have a panic attack.

As she started talking to me about the company and how she hopes it will improve in the future, my mind started to wander.

Earl: What the hell have you done?

Me: I don't know!

Earl: You've quit your job?? You're not going to have any income and there's a cost-of-living crisis and you live in an expensive part of England and have a flat to pay for and what if they put the rent up and you can't afford it but you also can't afford to rent anywhere else because everywhere else requires you to actually have a job in order to prove that you can afford said flat? What have you done?!

Me: Shit.

Earl: Take it back. Tell her you've changed your mind and you'll stay, you'll even take a pay cut.

Wanda: This is fantastic, Jenna! You've waited for this day for years and you're finally taking charge of your life. What a brilliant opportunity you have to really live your dream!

Earl: You've never dreamt of being homeless before.

Me: I've done it now – I just have to go along with it, it will work out.

Wanda: Exactly! God, this is so exciting, you're going to absolutely smash this!!

My dream (for those who want me to paint them a picture) includes me living in a shit-hot amazing house on the beach, writing full-time (well, I say full-time, but let's say that I want to be working part-time hours for full-time pay, #UnderworkedAndOverpaid), owning at *least* one cockapoo who is obsessed with me but also likes spending time on her own and who doesn't mind me leaving the house for drinks of an evening with my millions of friends who laugh at all of my jokes.

I'll also be off on at least three foreign holidays a year – one epic long-haul, one European and one somewhere in the middle where I'll be paid a stupid amount of money by some magazine or publisher to write about my trip. I'll also win my tennis club's summer tournament (alright, Jenna, let's be realistic, yeah?).

So that is my dream and as you can see, it all starts with *the writing*. You'll also notice that I didn't include a wife/partner/sex friend in that dream because I'm working on *me*. If I can be 100 per cent happy with just me, then anyone who is lucky enough to *have* me (my friend's words, not mine) will get the best Jenna they can get and not some codependent shadow of a woman who is just looking for someone to complete her.

The news keeps telling me there's a cost-of-living crisis, that council tax, food and other essentials are going up in price and basically, the country is going to be well and truly screwed for the next few years. So, sure, it's not the 'best' time to quit my job and make it as a writer, but when is a good time?

> **Wanda:** The best time to do anything is right now!
> **Me:** Well, not *anything*, it's obviously not the right time to travel to Ukraine.
> **Earl:** The war in Ukraine is a reminder that life is dire and humans are—
> **Wanda & Me:** Shut up, Earl.

I've saved up enough money to keep me going for five months and that'll give me enough time to write my book (this one in your hands, that you're hopefully enjoying), and if it doesn't work out then I can just go back to the daily grind until I'm able to try again.

If this year has taught me anything, it's that, a) it *was* all the carbs that was making me fat, b) it's important to watch the ball when playing tennis and, c) just because you're scared of something, it doesn't mean you can't do it.

If you're scared of doing something, then just do it scared. Unless it's doing heart surgery, in which case, don't do it. Step away from the scalpel.

CHAPTER 40

ANY FIVE FOOT TEN PARAMEDICS IN THE HOUSE?

Jamie and Josie came over on Saturday and encouraged me (read: bullied me) to download Tinder. But to be fair there wasn't much encouragement needed, because even though I don't want to go on any dates just yet, I would like to see what will be on the menu come the day that I am ready.

Just to let you know that *of course* I am not objectifying women by saying that they are items on a menu, but dating and women scare me, so if I can refer to them as something that doesn't scare me, aka food, then it makes it easier for me to deal with. So less of your judgement, please.

'I think it's time you started dating again,' Jamie said after she finished the banging prawn linguine I'd made (with a side salad, rather than a huge slab of garlic bread because weight-loss goals, darling).

'Why?' I replied.

'Well, because quite frankly I'm beyond bored of hearing about your breakup. You need some new problems. Do you know what breeds new problems? Dating. So, we're doing your Tinder profile.'

SCREWED UP, SLIMMED DOWN

'But I'm happy being single.'

'Oh, you're happy to never have sex again are you?' I opened my mouth to reply and then closed it again. 'Thought so. Right, let's begin. So, what sort of woman are you looking for?' she asked.

'I'm looking for an athletic blonde paramedic who's obsessed with giving massages,' I replied.

'Oh, darling, I think we're going to have to lower our expectations. OK, so what are we looking for. Minimum height?'

'Five foot ten.'

'Five foot,' Jamie said, entering the details into the app. 'Preferred location?'

'Anywhere within five miles.'

'300 miles.' She continued to edit. 'And finally, profession – you said paramedic, would you accept Tesco worker?'

'Sure.'

'Of course you would. Now, let's do your profile.'

'Oh God.'

'Height?' Jamie asked.

'Five foot nine.'

'Even with your humpback? Huh… What are your interests? And don't say tennis, no one gives a fuck about your fucking tennis.'

'I like reading.'

'Boring.'

'Writing.'

'Eugh.'

'I also like having drunken existential debates with myself late at night.'

'There we go! Bit psychotic,' Jamie typed.

'You can't put that.'

'…But not psychotic *enough* as to actually be sectioned. Happy?'

'Can you also put that I'm very caring, am emotionally stable and would treat someone like a queen?' I asked.

SCREWED UP, SLIMMED DOWN

Jamie raised a single eyebrow.

'No, that sounds like you're a desperate little puppy with mummy issues. And we both know that you're anything but emotionally stable. OK, let's summarise. You're looking for a five foot Tesco worker from the general England area and in return you can offer reading, writing and drunken existential debates late at night. Sound good?'

I took the phone off her, entered the *correct* details and started to swipe my way through the app. Surprisingly, there were a lot of couples looking for a threesome. Bitch, please, I can only just about satisfy one other person, let alone *two*. I continued to swipe.

'Nope, she's too pretty.' Swipe. 'She's too hot.' Swipe. 'She's too weird. She's got kids and she's a smoker,' I said, swiping away.

'Any that you do like, bbz?' Jamie asked.

'Oh, this lady is beautiful, and she likes tennis!'

'Win!'

'Oh, but she likes coffee.'

'What's wrong with that?' Josie asked.

'I don't like coffee.'

'You don't have to like it,' Josie pointed out.

'No, but it starts at coffee – what else don't we have in common? Also, one of her interests is the theatre. Bore off.'

I did swipe right on a couple of women, but as this was my first time on a dating app for nine years I may have had my standards raised to maximum.

Ten minutes after Jamie and Josie left I had completed Tinder and matched with two people, both of whom live over 20 miles away. Well, it's a bloody good job that I'm happy living the single life at the moment…

CHAPTER 41

THE BEST DAY OF THE YEAR

November

'I don't want to go and stay at their house for the weekend, I just want to go to the party and then leave,' I told my therapist during last week's session.

'OK, then I'm going to ask you a question,' she said. I always know a really deep challenging question is coming when she announces that she's going to ask a question before actually asking it. 'If you don't want to stay at their house, then why *are* you staying?'

I thought for a moment. Oh yeah, why *am* I staying at my brother's house after my dad's 70th birthday party if I don't want to? I mean, I *really* don't want to – it's nothing to do with my brother, it's because the last time I stayed at his was when I was with Cat and I had that massive panic attack.

'Because I'm expected to,' I replied eventually.

'And what would happen if you *didn't* stay?' she asked.

'My brother wouldn't be very happy, he'd probably be disappointed.'

'So you'd rather disappoint yourself than disappoint others?'

'Yeah. But that's what I've always done, I've always put

others' happiness and comfort levels before my own.'

'And how has that worked for you?' she asked with a smile on her face, because by this point I was smirking at how ridiculous I sounded.

'Not very well,' I laughed.

My therapist and I have these wonderful moments of realisation at least once per session where I tell her something, she then asks me questions to get to the root of what I've said, and then she lands this big truth bomb. I always end up laughing at how it's taken me this long to realise that, a) it's what I've been doing all my life and, b) it's probably why I've not been the happiest little bunny I can be.

Throughout my life I've been so busy trying to make other little bunnies happy that I haven't bothered trying to make *myself* happy – this makes me feel sad and I don't want to be a sad little bunny anymore! I want to be a great big walloping happy bunny with a huge fluffy tail.

One of my biggest problems that I've recently learnt about from my fabulous therapist (I promise I'm not just calling her that because she laughs at my jokes) is that I try to get my happiness, self-esteem and self-worth *externally*. And as we all know (or at least, I do *now*), external things can't be relied upon because they change. E.g. people, places and animals – people turn into dicks, places become too familiar and animals get sick and die (I haven't broken this news to Rusty and Tiny Tim just yet).

'What would it be like if you could get your self-worth from yourself?' she asked.

'It would be amazing, I'd be able to be myself with everyone 100 per cent, I would do the things that make me happy and not what's expected. And I would feel content and not in a constant state of lack,' I replied, making my therapist smile.

Since the beginning of the year my self-worth has definitely been improving, due to me being more my authentic self and having more confidence by getting out of my comfort zone – I'm now even able to do things without worrying about what other people think. For example, I was in the cinema on my own the other day and there was no one else there until these two old ladies came in.

'Oh, Deirdre, we've got the cinema to ourselves,' one of them said to the other, who might have been a 'Deirdre', but to be fair she could've been a 'Sharon', it was difficult to tell.

I then had a split second to decide whether to, a) slide down my seat and pretend that I wasn't there or, b) wave and say a big cheery hello.

'Hello!' I waved at them, to which they looked up and waved back.

'Oh, hello,' they said. 'Wouldn't it be funny if we came and sat right next to you?'

No, Deirdre or Sharon, it would *not* be funny, it would be *lovely*, I'd love the company… That's a lie, obviously what they needed to do was sit on the opposite side of the cinema because those are the unspoken rules of society. Luckily, that's what they did – well played, old ladies.

'So how was the party at your brother's house?' my therapist asked me after I'd got back from my dad's birthday party at the weekend.

'It was fine, it wasn't anywhere near as bad as I thought it would be. I didn't have a panic attack, my brother and his husband didn't say too many things to wind me up and I left when I was ready at 8:30 pm.'

I'd just like you to know that the party started at 4 pm, so although leaving a party at 8:30 pm *sounds* like it's super early, it's not. I usually like to leave parties about 9 pm, which I find is the earliest acceptable time that I can leave without someone asking me if I'm not well.

There was a moment during the party when my dad started opening his birthday presents in front of everyone, and my brother's husband learnt that one of the presents I'd bought him was a colander – yes, it's a weird gift and

SCREWED UP, SLIMMED DOWN

not one that I particularly would've liked for my dad to open in front of everyone, but when your dad asks for a colander for his birthday, you buy him a colander.

'Open that one! Open that one!' my brother-in-law cried out multiple times while jumping up and down and pointing at the wrapped gift. I knew that he was just doing that so that I'd be embarrassed and everyone would laugh at me and when my dad *did* open it everyone *did* laugh, including me. My dad put the colander on his head like the silly buffoon he is, and I wasn't embarrassed in the *slightest*. I owned the moment instead of being made to feel stupid, because I no longer give other people the power to make me feel like an idiot. I can do that on my own, thanks, I don't need any help.

'That's great. So you didn't stay the night and nothing bad happened, what does that tell you?' my therapist asked.

'That things aren't ever as bad as I think they're going to be,' I replied. 'However, on the same day as my dad's party it was Cat's birthday and I learnt via Jamie that she went to Barcelona with FKA Bitch Face for the weekend and I got a pang of anxiety.'

'Why did you get anxiety?'

'Because I suddenly thought, "Oh God, they're having this amazing exciting weekend away having all the sex and here I am watching a man put a colander on his head."' We both laughed. 'But then I went on Cat's Facebook profile to see a picture of the two of them together and suddenly the anxiety and dread disappeared. It was like I'd taken the plug out of the bath full of water and the fact that she has a new girlfriend doesn't hurt anymore.'

'Wow,' my therapist said, which always makes me happy because I want to impress her with how much growth I've made. I aim for at least one 'wow' per session.

For the rest of the session we spoke about how I catastrophise things. To me, things are either terrible or amazing – but she told me that life is somewhere in between. This is *good* news, but this also *bad* news. I'll tell you for why.

It's *good*, because it means that nothing is ever going to be as bad as I think it's going to be. For example, I thought that my dad's birthday party was going to be spent with me answering people's questions about my breakup, having to explain myself about why I didn't want to stay and then having an awful argument with my brother where he ends up banning me from the house. But nothing like that happened.

However, it's also *bad*, because it means that reality can never live up to my fantasy/expectation of it. For example, when I was going to move to Edinburgh everything was going to be amazing and shiny and oh so orgasmic – but actually if I *had* moved there I soon would've realised that my expectations of the place weren't realistic, and I would've been left feeling hopeless because I'd bet all of my happiness on the move working out.

'Sometimes people cast their net of happiness out so far that it's hard for them to get the things that make them happy,' my therapist began. 'For example, if you think you're *only* going to be happy once you live in a certain area, or you've got the dream house, the perfect job, partner and social life, then you won't be happy *until* you get those things. Which will make the everyday *unhappy*,' she said.

'And also, those big things probably won't live up to my crazy expectations anyway!' I chimed in. Is it OK to use the word 'crazy' during therapy? What about 'hullaballoo'?

'Exactly. So if we can learn to cast our net of happiness a little nearer, so focusing on friends, music, writing and tennis; things that we can add to our *everyday* lives – then we can learn to be a lot happier right now,' she said, imitating a small fishing net being thrown from a boat.

This is *very* true, because the other day I had the best day that I've had in ages, even though nothing very

SCREWED UP, SLIMMED DOWN

extraordinary happened – I didn't even win the lottery or have the most mind-blowing sex with Kate Winslet.

There I was on just a regular Thursday morning, doing some writing while watching the rain thrash against my window, when suddenly Louise texted me asking to play badminton later.

We played badminton and it was fun and she didn't totally thrash me (though don't ask her about that). After which I went home, had lunch and then my friend Steve from the tennis club texted me asking if I could help him move his dismantled kitchen into the back of his van. He certainly knows a strapping lesbian when he sees one.

I then helped him with his kitchen, did a bit of food shopping and ended the day playing some banging tennis and chatting with all of my lovely tennis friends.

'I have had the best day *ever*. It was fun, it was light, I didn't overthink, it was normal, I saw some of the most special friends I've made this year, I played tennis and I am *so* happy right now,' I said to myself, beaming on the car ride home from tennis.

'And what was the main reason why you had such a good day?' my therapist asked.

'I didn't overthink or analyse everything – I did my favourite things, I spent time with my favourite people and I was just in the present.'

'Wow,' she said, nodding slowly.

Woo hoo, two 'wows' in one session! I should get a special sticker or something.

Due to me being an unemployed bum right now I can only afford to see my therapist every fortnight, but she is worth *every* penny. Though obviously, I'm not going to tell *her* that, or she might put her rates up.

CHAPTER 42

THIRTY-EIGHT INCHES OF PURE SEX APPEAL

When I put my mind to something I (mostly, on occasion) achieve it. And that's what's happened this year with the weight-loss thing, as I'm now down to 13 stone 3 pounds, which is just three pounds away from having lost three stone this year – and six overall since my flabbyist. I'm so incredibly proud of my achievement that I might go and celebrate with some chocolate.

> **Wanda:** No, Jenna. You're doing so well!
> **Me:** I'm joking! Keep your bra on.
> **Wanda:** I don't have a bra, I'm just a voice in your head.
> **Me:** Ew, there's a braless voice inside my head.
> **Earl:** That's what you're weirded out about? Well, in that case it's probably a good time to tell you that I'm not wearing any pants.

It's one week until my birthday and I'm aiming to get down to that elusive 13 stone by then. So, one week and three pounds to lose – I can totally do it! I've already

SCREWED UP, SLIMMED DOWN

gotten down to my goal belly-circumference measurement of 38 inches. Yes, you can put this book down to get your tape measure out to see how rotund a 38 inch belly is.

My weekly videos about my weight loss are getting more and more popular; one even has over a million views. Am I rich yet? No, but have I had a few sexy ladies slide into my DMs? Yes, a few…

I'm still working on myself and it's going great. Sure, I still get those sad moments that turn into anger, which then turns into exhaustion, which then turns into excellent fodder for comedy videos, but they're happening less and less.

There's just one and a half months left of this transformation year and I must keep this momentum going!

CHAPTER 43

THE FIRST BIRTHDAY ON MY OWN

I don't mean to be dramatic, but everything is awful and the world is shit.

'I don't want to be here anymore,' I said to myself last night as I sat in my car crying my eyes out along Hove seafront. 'I want to drink myself into oblivion, I want to drive 100mph into a wall, I just don't want to be here anymore!' If you can't tell, I was a tad bit upset... Let's cut back to a few hours earlier in the day to see *why* I was so full of all the feelings.

Jamie and Josie's wedding is coming up in less than a month and it's going to be a very small wedding and Cat is going to be there, so in order for us to avoid looking like a pair of awkward gooses I texted her suggesting that we meet up for a coffee/tea a couple of days before. Five hours after I'd texted her she replied saying that she didn't think FKA Bitch Face would like that. Oh, under the thumb already, are we?

Later on I received a voice message from Jamie saying that she'd spoken to Cat and it transpires that Cat has turned into a bit of a liar because actually FKA Bitch Face *doesn't* have a problem with it, but it's actually *Cat* that didn't want to meet because she didn't think it was necessary.

Oh, she didn't think it was necessary? Well, a) she's wrong, we need to put our friend's wedding before our own comfort levels, b) we're going to be in a room with just 18 other people, all of whom will be looking at us to see if there's any drama, SO LET'S MAKE SURE THERE'S NO DRAMA, and, c) what happened to us being friends eventually? If she can't even meet me for a tea without shitting her pants or thinking it's 'not necessary', then I don't see much hope for a nice friendship between us.

From a young age I've felt very unwanted, and no matter how much therapy I do, if someone says or does something to press that little 'no one cares about Jenna' button inside of me then I fall back into being an utter mess. My inner child gets triggered and I end up drowning in feelings of rejection and primal loneliness.

Sure, this is happening less frequently, but birthdays have *always* triggered this button and today was my birthday – the first one on my own in nine years. The first one where Cat wasn't here to make a huge song and dance of it and make me feel like a special princess.

Originally, I wanted to spend my birthday crying in bed on my own, but then I thought, 'No, that's the *old* Jenna.' So what I did instead was arrange to do all of my favourite things with all of my favourite people.

I was going to go for lunch with a friend, play badminton with another friend and then end the day at Jamie and Josie's with a dirty Chinese takeaway and some beers. It was two days ago that the lunch friend cancelled and it was last night that my badminton friend cancelled. Sure, these people didn't know how poignant this day was going to be for me, so their cancellation was just casual from their point of view, but to me, I felt disregarded – and that's why I was crying in my car.

Wanda: The lunch friend was busy with something at

work and the badminton friend wasn't well; it's not a reflection on you or your worth.

Me: Yeah, but…

Wanda: No buts, listen to what I'm saying and move on.

Earl: Ooooooh, who rattled her cage?

Wanda: You can shut it as well, Earl. Jenna, you're just feeling extra emotional because you're ovulating.

Me: I'm not ovulating…

OK, so maybe I am ovulating and yes, it does always makes me extra emotional, not to mention horny. Two quite conflicting feelings. My body is like, 'How best can we get some spermatozoa in here? I know, let's make her horny!' Yes, I get that bit, that makes sense, but why then do I need to be extra emotional to get the spermatozoa? Is that how straight relationships work? To stop the woman from being so emotional the man has sex with her? God, straight people are so weird.

The past few weeks have seen a big improvement in the mental health side of this transformational doodah, but last night felt like a big shitting step back.

'Healing is not a linear process,' my therapist has told me in the past, and after Googling what the hell linear means, I can see what she's saying.

OK, so last night was tough and a dip in my progress, but I'm still moving forward. Also, I didn't do any of those things that I felt like doing and instead I drove home, cuddled my fluffy children and wrote my feelings in my journal like the sensitive little bunny that I am.

This morning, on my 33rd birthday, I awoke with extremely puffy 'I cried all night' eyes, but I got up, took a long hard look in the mirror and promised that I was going to put my big-girl pants on and give myself the best birthday that I could.

During the day I took myself to Brighton and explored everything this gay little town has to offer, and I

SCREWED UP, SLIMMED DOWN

thoroughly enjoyed myself – even though it was so cold that my tits nearly froze off.

I went up the i360 – which is a big doughnut shaped viewing platform that goes 162 metres up into the air so that you can see what Brighton's rooftops look like. I had an ice cream on the pier – so that my insides could match my freezing outsides. I went to the Upside Down House on the beach – it's a house that's upside down so it looks like you're walking on the ceiling, literally *seconds* of fun… And I went to McDonald's to have some large fries and a cookie for lunch because it's my bloody birthday and 'Jenna's form of keto' doth not apply on my bloody birthday.

After exhausting everything Brighton has to offer (apart from all the drugs, I honestly don't need to give my mind any more things to deal with), I went to Jamie and Josie's house for a banging Chinese takeaway and a few delicious beers.

'What should I do about Cat? Shall I just see if she wants to be friends?' I asked them, four beers in.

'Hmm, let's unpack that,' Jamie said. 'Does she warrant your friendship at the moment?'

Who? How? What now? Does *she* warrant *my* friendship? Well, no, she's being a bit of a butthead at the moment, but like with all of my friendships, I don't think about whether *they* warrant *my* friendship. It's always, am *I* good enough for *them*?

'Oh my God, Jamie. How have I got to the age of 33 and only just realised this?'

'You didn't just realise this, I've just told you this. I'm taking the credit for this realisation,' she said, having a swig of her beer.

How mad is that? I think *so* little of myself that I am just happy with whoever wants to be my friend, regardless of whether I want *them* as a friend. Oh my God, this is going to be life-changing.

From now on I will only make and keep friends that

bring something into my life, they need to warrant *my* friendship and bother about *me* and not just when they want something. Holy mother of Jesus, this feels liberating! It also feels a bit 'Who the hell does Jenna think she is?' But that's just because you can't get rid of 33 years of conditioning over just one Chinese takeaway.

Now, as I sit on my living room floor slightly buzzed from the beer and the relief that the day I was dreading is over, I'm playing with my guinea pigs who (definitely *do not* warrant my friendship) make me feel happy and calm.

These little fluffy nubbins have kept me company during many evenings this year and, although having them has meant that I have to clean out their poo three times a week and put up with zero kisses in return, I am mighty glad that I won them in the divorce.

'Mummy is proud of herself today,' I told them earlier as I gave them their nightly spinach. 'She managed to get through this tough day and she realised that she doesn't need anyone else to make her feel like a princess, she can make herself feel like a princess, isn't that right, Rusty and Tiny Tim?' I smiled at them, half expecting them to answer but half hoping that they wouldn't because I know that as soon as the guinea pigs start talking back it's either time to get rid of them or get myself booked in to the Funny Farm.

Today proves that I don't need someone else to save me. I am, in the words of Destiny's Child, an independent woman.

'*I buy my own diamonds and I buy my own rings*' (but replace 'diamonds' with 'cookies' and 'rings' with 'fries').

CHAPTER 44

IT'S CALLED FASHION, DICKHEAD

Shopping, like sex, is best done on your own. After having lost three stone this year, I very much needed to buy myself some clothes that actually fit – I also needed a proper boob hammock that supports my boobs and doesn't just hang on my body like some saggy potato sack.

So, I booked myself in for a bra fitting at my local M&S, I shaved my armpits and moisturised my torso ready for someone to look at and feel my bahoobaboobers for the first time in seven months. However, to my utter disappointment when I got to the bra fitting yesterday there was a big sign on the wall that read, 'You can keep your clothes on, you dirty pervert,' or something to that effect.

'When did you last have your bra fitted?' the shop assistant asked as she put the freezing cold measuring tape around my chest below my existing bra.

'Six stone ago,' I replied smugly.

'Oh wow, and how long did that take you to lose?'

'It's taken six years, but I've done three stone in this year alone,' I said, still smug as a prize pig even though I was standing there in my baggy three-year-old bra with my belly out.

'OK, so you're definitely not a 40F anymore, I'd probably say you're a 38DD. I'll go and get you some bras to try on, you want black underwired one with lace, yes?' she asked.

'Wow, how did you know that just by looking at me?' I gasped.

'You wrote it on the form when you made the online booking.' Oh yeah… 'It's also what you're wearing now.'

Wow, what an idiot.

Once I'd tried on the bras that the assistant got me and I pretended that I was going to actually buy them (who the hell can afford M&S? Not this unemployed bum, that's for sure), I went clothes shopping for Jamie and Josie's wedding, an event where there will be a ton of very hot lesbians, so I'd need to look as banging as possible.

While I was doing the clothes shopping, I bumped into Louise and she, ever the very thin woman that she is, showed me the pyjama set that she was buying.

'I'm a size 14,' she said. I've not got a scoob what size I am in the women's department. In the men's I'm now a sexy Medium (I don't know if I've mentioned that before).

'You need to add more colour to your wardrobe,' she said.

'No, I don't, I'm the lesbian Johnny Cash.'

'You're the lesbian idiot,' she replied.

I did try on a bright orange ladies' dress to see what I looked like in colour and it turns out that orange goes well with my Mediterranean complexion – it really brings out the mania in my eyes. Also… I'm a size 14. Woo hoo! I'm not entirely sure how I'm the same size as Louise, considering she's two stone lighter than me, but who am I to argue with M&S and their generous sizing?

It wasn't long before I swapped the colourful crap for some black men's attire: a black waistcoat, black trousers, black shirt and a black tux jacket. Louise can sod off with her colour. Sorry, bbz.

As I stood there in the changing room in my sexy new

SCREWED UP, SLIMMED DOWN

all-black outfit I smiled to myself. There's no feeling quite like putting on some clothes and thinking, 'Yeah, I look and feel good in this.' When you're seven stone overweight, like I was a few years ago, you dream of having these moments but you think that they'll never actually happen. You think you're just destined to be fat and wear tents forever.

Looking back at photos of me from years ago, it was very clear that I had an identity crisis. In some photos, I was wearing hoop earrings and lady blouses with men's combats and boots. I was clearly confused; who should I be? Who am I *expected* to be? By nature, I'm a people-pleaser who just tries to adapt herself to fit in with whoever she's with. It's funny to me now as I look back at how I've been and acted in certain friendships and relationships. I can see I was playing a part, even with my dress sense.

Well, no more. I am Jenna and if I want to wear a man's black waistcoat with Doctor Martens and short dykey hair, then I will – because that's the real Jenna and she looks and *feels* fabulous in it.

'Bollocks to it, I'm going to treat myself,' I thought as I bought the shiny tuxedo jacket from M&S. Obviously, I kept the receipt so that I can take it back after the wedding. Please, I can't afford to go splashing £80 on a tuxedo jacket that I'll only wear once.

CHAPTER 45

I CAN FILL UP MY OWN CUP, THANK YOU

December
Today I had another ridiculously excellent therapy session. We started by talking about the ladies' Christmas tennis tournament that I went to last night, where I was completely myself and I didn't just spend the entire evening caring what other people thought of me. Yes, the tennis was significantly below par, but authentic Jenna? She was on form!

After we'd played the tennis tournament we all went into the clubhouse to enjoy the buffet food that everyone had brought, which was made up of 12 quiches that no one ate, a million sausage rolls and a selection of desserts including chocolate eclairs, chocolate cake and chocolate brownies.

Did I just sit there scoffing all the chocolate pretending that I was too busy eating to participate in conversation? No, I downed my chocolate quickly and contributed to *multiple* conversations – I even chatted with the scary women at the club who I used to avoid because I thought they were too uppity to communicate with the likes of me.

SCREWED UP, SLIMMED DOWN

But I *did* communicate with these women, I even made jokes and I was 100 per cent myself.

'That brownie is looking at me,' I said to one woman while pointing at the last brownie.

'Have it,' she said.

'But I've already had two, that'll be my third.'

'Your third!' she said, sounding genuinely shocked. Bitch, please, if no one else was here I would've inhaled all three in two seconds.

'I know! Step away from the brownies, Jenna…' I said, stepping away but still salivating.

A few minutes passed and someone else picked up the last brownie – thank God, I really want to lose these last few pounds before the year is out, I'm so close to getting under 13 stone.

'Did you have three?!' the other woman shrieked, looking at the empty plate.

'No, I absolutely did not! How dare you suggest such a thing… Julie got there before me, she's the pig!' I replied, which made her burst out laughing.

Now, I'm not saying that me and this woman are kindred spirits who are going to become besties, but the small genuine connection in this tiny exchange (and multiple other exchanges during the course of the evening) felt amazing. The feeling of being accepted for being your true self is really rather wonderful and it's a mighty shame that I've waited until the age of 33 to start doing it. I'm going to try being myself with everyone now, I might even try cracking a joke at the bin men and see how that goes down.

'Oh, you're a writer?' one of the new women at the club asked me last night as I shoved more cake into my gob. I could tell that, a) she was gay (yay), b) she was married (boo) and, c) we looked like we could be friends, because aesthetically we look very similar – we're both in our 30s, we both have short hair and we both like tennis and women.

'Yeah, I write comedy sketches and books about mental health and lesbian culture,' I told her, finally not afraid to tell people about my work.

'Oh great, how can I find your stuff?' she asked.

'Just put my name into Facebook and you will find my page with all my videos and books,' I said, not giving her my surname because she'd only forget it. But she knows that my name is Jenna and I'm a lesbian, so I'm sure if she were to type those two words into Google, I'd come up.

Just as the delightful evening was coming to a close and I was heading towards the door to leave, the new woman came up to me.

'So what's your surname for me to find you online?' she asked. Sorry, what now? You're actually genuinely interested in my silly little writing and comedy videos? No, it's OK, I've shown interest in you, you don't need to go above and beyond to pretend that you're interested in me in return. Oh, unless you are? Oh, yay, she actually *is* genuinely interested in me – not in that way obviously because she's married and I'm not quite ready to bump doughnuts with anyone just yet. But yay, someone wants to know more about what I do!

To some of you reading this who haven't tried to hide yourself for most of your life, this may sound like a load of absolute twatting waffle, but when you have worn a mask for decades and then taken it off and actually been accepted and not rejected by others, well, it's just bloody wonderful and life-affirming. Genuine human connection, eh? There's nothing quite like it.

'Wow,' my therapist said, looking at me in wonder after I finished telling her about the evening. No, I wasn't just telling her about my amazing growth *just* to make her go 'wow', thank you very much… I don't need my therapist to validate me. I'm learning to get my validation from myself now – I mean, suuuuuuure, if someone else wants to make me feel validated as well, then that's lovely. But only if they're validating my *true* self and not my fake masked people-pleasing self.

Towards the middle of today's therapy session I told her about the mini crisis I'd had in my car the night before my birthday, where I'd cried my eyes out, feeling so unwanted and unloved. My therapist did what I pay her to do – she made me feel better about the situation. Obviously, if you were to ask my therapist if it's her job to make me feel better, she would say no.

'So, I'm going to turn that on its head,' she began. 'You felt unwanted and unloved and that's really difficult. But you *felt* that and it was real and you didn't repress it, you *felt* it.' Does she mean to say that I'm growing and not repressing my feelings anymore? Fan-dabby-dozy!

'Your feelings should tell you that the people who you're looking to make you feel loved and wanted aren't able to. For whatever reason, they *can't* do that. And it's not that you aren't lovable, it's that they can't give you the love you need. So, perhaps you need to not put all your focus on the people who *can't* make you feel loved and look for those who *can,*' she said, using her hands to emphasise the point more.

Oh shit, yeah… It's *not* that I'm unlovable – I'm nice, I'm funny, I'm extremely considerate and I *am* lovable. It's that these people can't make me feel how I want them to. But that's OK because, a) it's not their job to make me feel how I want and, b) I'm learning to fill up my *own* cup and one day the actions of others won't trigger my inner child quite so much.

The night before my birthday was tough but it was short-lived, which shows that even though this healing process is up and down, it's still going in the right direction.

'I just want to quickly talk about how I'm going to deal with my friend's wedding,' I said 10 minutes before our session finished.

'OK, what are your feelings around it?' my therapist asked.

SCREWED UP, SLIMMED DOWN

'I know that I'm going to be subconsciously looking out for Cat texting her girlfriend.'

'So her girlfriend isn't going to the wedding?'

'No, plus there's only 20 people at the wedding, so there's not really anywhere to hide.'

'OK, so what is it about her texting her girlfriend that is going to make you feel bad? Is it that she looks like she's happy and OK?'

'Yeah.'

'But, you're also happy and OK. Yes, you don't have all the parts of the life you want yet in terms of a girlfriend, but you're being your authentic self, you're having fun, you're doing your writing and you're still losing weight and putting yourself first. She might have this girlfriend, but let's keep focusing on what *you* have and not what you *don't* have.'

'God, you're right.'

'Also, we don't know what mask Cat will be wearing. Maybe she's going to find the day difficult as well, so she might text her girlfriend more to give her some comfort.'

'That's true.'

'I'd be interested to know,' she went on, 'what if this wedding had happened back in January when you were still with Cat? What if the current Jenna sitting in front of me were to walk into the wedding and see old Jenna? How would that look?'

My eyes instantly filled with hot tears. Holy shit. Old Jenna… old, chubby, unhappy, burdened, anxiety-filled, panic-attack-having Jenna.

'Oh my God… If I walked into the wedding and I saw old Jenna I would feel so sorry for her, I would want to hug her and tell her that it *does* get better.'

'And what would old Jenna think if she were to see the new Jenna you've become?' my therapist asked as the tears started to fall from my eyes.

'She would look at me, look at all the progress I've made and then she would say, "That looks amazing, but that's *impossible*, I can never become that person.'"

My therapist's eyes started to well up a bit as she grabbed her chest. 'Wow, that feels so poignant and meaningful.'

Holy hell, what an *utterly* profound moment in therapy. If I look back at the old Jenna in January who was sitting in that hypnotherapy session, I can see that she was *so* unhappy and burdened that she couldn't see a way out. And this Jenna, this current Jenna *is* that future Jenna that I imagined within the trance who came out of the super big cinema system and gave me the green precious stone.

Wow... It would seem that all of this hard work has been worth it. Thank fuck for that.

CHAPTER 46

TWELVE STONE AND 13 POUNDS OF FABULOUSNESS

I've done it! I'm finally under 13 stone for the first time in nine years! Maybe I *can* finish this year strong. I haven't felt this good about myself for so long. This year really has been my year, even though at times it felt like the absolute shitting pits.

There's just three weeks of the year left and I need to lose another six pounds and two inches around my belly in order to get down to my goal of 12 stone 7 pounds and 37 inches of belly fabulousness. Let's hope nothing gets in my way! (And by 'nothing' I obviously mean Christmas, New Year and the wedding.)

CHAPTER 47

GOODBYE MY FLUFFY LITTLE NUBBIN

My sweet little Rusty has died. The little ginger fluffy nubbin that has been there for me throughout this tough year (much to his annoyance), has left me just two weeks before Christmas – the little prick.

He had an inoperable lump in his stomach for quite some time, but recently it had gotten bigger and it was clearly causing him pain because he wasn't being his usual self; he wasn't moving as much, he wasn't eating as much and he wasn't giving me his death stare quite as much either. As a guinea pig mother, when you know, you *know*.

'We're just going to sort out what we need to, so we'll give you a few minutes alone with him,' the vet said softly as she left me and Rusty alone in the consulting room.

'I'm so sorry, my darling,' I wept into him as I rocked him in my arms. My little google bear who grew into his big froggy eyes was leaving me and going up to guinea pig heaven (which sounds amazing, I hope I get to go there when I die).

I handed him over to the vet, paid the receptionist £104 (if that's what it costs to get into guinea pig heaven

SCREWED UP, SLIMMED DOWN

then actually I think I'll pass) and made my way very quickly to my car trying my best not to let the floodgate of tears burst open before I got there. I didn't want to be there when the vet gave him the injection, I didn't want to see him take his last breath – that's way too much for such a delicate little bunny like me to see.

Cat had texted me while I was in the vet's arranging tomorrow's 'let's not make our friend's wedding awkward' coffee/tea catch-up. But I knew that I wouldn't be able to face it after just losing Rusty, so I sent her a voice message explaining what had just happened at the vets. And then she called me…

It was so nice to hear her voice, to hear a comforting voice from someone who knew how much Rusty meant to me.

It's really interesting how people react differently to death, especially the death of a pet. Those without pets or who don't understand that they are not just something to fill your house with but are actually *preferred* members of your family just don't get it. These types of people would be more concerned to hear that your TV had broken down.

But then there are some wonderful people who *truly* get it and one of them was my friend Steve from tennis who texted me saying:

'Oh no, so sorry to hear that. If you need a garden he is welcome to rest in peace here. The others send their love too. Xoxoxo'. Oh, such kindness from someone who I don't really know all that well yet.

Tiny Tim (my last remaining guinea pig) isn't a big fan of cuddles, so he's not particularly appreciated the extra fuss I've been making of him this week, but guinea pigs aren't meant to be on their own (it's even illegal in Switzerland to have only one guinea pig), so I need to make sure he doesn't get too lonely before I take him to meet his new guinea pig family next week.

That's what I've felt these past 24 hours – a harrowing

loneliness. I'm on my own, I'm doing all of this on my own, it's another 'first' that I have to deal with… First birthday, first time I blocked the toilet and had to unclog it on my own, and now the first death.

Rusty's death and Tiny Tim going to a new family is so symbolic because they were the last thing left from my life with Cat (apart from the Dyson, but *obviously* I'm never parting with that). As much as I would've loved to keep Tiny Tim, it wouldn't be fair on him to be on his own and I can't afford to get another guinea pig; they cost a lot in food and upkeep and also, if you keep replacing the dead guinea pigs then you end up with perpetual guinea pigs.

I popped to the shops today to get supplies for me and Tiny Tim and as I stared at the huge bars of Christmas-themed chocolate (for like, a good 20 minutes), I decided that I wouldn't do what I normally do and buy a shitload of chocolate and 'feel-good' food to get me through this pain.

The feel-good food doesn't make me feel good, it makes me feel crap. And if I'm going to keep improving myself and showing up for myself then I need to continue to put my health first. Therefore, I just got a caramel Freddo – 25p for a tiny chocolate bar is piss-poor value, especially during this economic crisis, but there's no feeling like trying on some clothes that were once too tight and are now too baggy.

Rusty's death has triggered a bit of the existential death anxiety similar to what I was experiencing at the beginning of the year. I'm not in full panic-attack mode by any stretch of the imagination, but there is a little murmur of anxiety deep within my gut. I know these feelings will pass, I just have to let them go through me.

Eckhart Tolle's book *The Power of Now* has been helping me a lot. It teaches you to focus on the now; focusing on what happened in the past or what *might* happen in the future will mean that you miss the present, and that's all we ever have. *Right here. Right now.*

SCREWED UP, SLIMMED DOWN

Once I've finished doing all this navel-gazing, *cough* I mean 'the amazing work on myself' I'm going to put it to good use by living life to the max and focusing on the positive things *outside* of myself. Obviously, I needed to do all the work within myself *first*, otherwise all the external stuff would've gone to shit, but I'm getting to a point where I have done enough internal work to be able to go dating, go travelling and really enjoy what life has to offer. Aka, me eating doughnuts on the beach with Kate Winslet on one side and a pen of guinea pigs on the other side, ahh, now that's *my* kind of heaven.

CHAPTER 48

A BIG LEZZY WEDDING

'Ladies and gentlemen, can you please be upstanding for the brides!' the registrar announced as Jamie and her dad walked down the aisle followed shortly by Josie and her best friend, who was giving her away. There I was, sitting on the second row next to Cat, both of us already drowning in tears. The wedding was finally here. Cat and I had ended our no-contact rule that had begun after we had got home from our post-breakup American holibobs and finally we had come together to watch our friends exchange their wedding vows. Vows that they wrote themselves and made even the coldest fish in the room cry.

A few days before the ceremony Cat and I agreed to do a video call for our 'let's not make our friend's wedding awkward' coffee/tea catch-up rather than meet in person due to me still being quite upset about my little Rusty's passing. So three days ago we had the catch-up and it went bloody swimmingly.

'Did your sister say that she's not going to do Christmas presents again this year?'

'Yup. Is your brother still complaining about the gyms being closed during Covid?'

SCREWED UP, SLIMMED DOWN

'You bet. Nothing changes.'

'Nothing changes.'

We caught up about our work situations, how our respective family dramas were going and how I've finally gotten rid of that verruca that I've had on my foot for 10 years.

'How are you and FKA Bitch Face?' I asked, genuinely interested.

'We're really good, I'm happy,' she replied. As I watched her say those words I felt such warmth and love for her. Yes, I was once madly in love with this woman and here she was telling me that she's happy with someone else, but I couldn't make her happy anymore so I'm truly glad that she's having all the sex and amazing times with someone else.

All the anger, anxiety and hurt that had poisoned me during our breakup was gone and I'm now in a place where I'm actually over the moon for Cat – I *want* for it to all work out for her. This is so good for me. I know, it's not all about me, but whatevs. Growth, darling, I'm all about it.

During this past week I've been dealing with a few different things; speaking to Cat again, the death of my little Rusty-bum, having to give Tiny Tim away and also mentally preparing for this wedding where I have to spend the whole love-themed day with my ex. If life was going to give me a challenge to test how much growth I've actually done, then *this* was going to be it.

On the morning of the wedding I was full of joy and excitement as I danced and sang along to a medley of P!nk songs while I washed and shaved all my bits in the shower. This time exactly two years ago I was getting ready for my brother's wedding and that morning was *very* different. That morning was spent with me crying in the bath having an existential crisis and telling my mum that I couldn't go to the wedding because I felt so awful. I was nearly morbidly obese, full of despair and stuck powerless in my own unhappy mental pit of poo. But now I'm just one stone overweight, am a lot happier and am no longer at the mercy of Earl and his unhappy mental pit of poo. In fact, most days I don't hear from him at all – I'm finally free!

Jamie and Josie's ceremony was beautiful and touching, and after it finished Cat and I went back to their house to set up the scene with Christmas lights and let the caterers in while the rest of the guests enjoyed a drink at a fancy bar. As we drove through Brighton high street (avoiding all the day drunks who like to run out in front of cars because playing chicken in traffic is most Brightonians' favourite pastime), we chatted about the ceremony, about her job, about my writing and what was going to happen to little Rusty's body. We were finally the friends we said we were going to be.

The wedding reception was held at the brides' house which meant that alcohol was free and bloody everywhere, so to celebrate the new happy friendship that Cat and I have found, I started to drink. A lot…

Tina Turner's *Simply the Best* was the first dance song and once the brides had done their short choreographed section they did the classic thing of 'We've done our dancy bit now you guys join in and stop gawking at us like we're in a zoo.' Cat made a beeline for me and we danced together, holding hands, smiling at each other with me twirling her around just like I used to. The laws of physics mean that she can't twirl me around because I'm five foot nine, and she's the height of a chicken, but that didn't matter because it was still lovely and it felt just like old times – in a happy non-sentimental way, of course. We had found our new way of being happy, separately but together.

Well, that was until half an hour later when she changed and spent the rest of the night avoiding all eye contact with me. I'd walk up to her and the group she was chatting with and she would just walk away like I was a bad smell that kept following her around. I was perplexed. Had

I done something wrong? Had I drunkenly said something stupid? I don't remember even saying *anything* to her after the first dance... Then why do I feel like my inner child has been triggered again?

Suddenly emotions flooded me and I felt lost, untethered and way too drunk. It'd been a very difficult week mentally, and now here Cat was being cold to me again.

Earl: What's her problem?

Me: I don't know? I've clearly done something wrong... oh God, I feel so sad.

Earl: She clearly doesn't care about you anymore and just wants to avoid you at all costs.

Wanda: Or! It's been tough for her to see you all day and now she needs a bit of a break.

Me: I don't know if I can keep it together much longer, but it's only 8:30 pm.

Earl: You can't leave! The brides will think you're an absolute bitch! Stay and drink more... Let's watch to see if Cat calls her girlfriend.

Wanda: Jenna, darling, if it's getting too much, then leave. You need to do what's best for you.

Me: But my friends might hate me.

Wanda: But if you stay you'll end up crying and getting more emotional. Put yourself first, darling. I'm sure your friends will understand.

I looked around and saw everyone dancing, drinking, laughing, smoking and having arm-wrestling competitions. But I just couldn't get out of my funk – the tears and anxiety were rising up.

'Are you OK to come and pick me up at 8:45 pm please?' I texted Louise.

'Yup, see you then.'

I hugged and kissed Jamie and Josie quickly; I knew that I might have to explain myself the next day, but I had to do what was right for me right then and that was it. I was putting myself first, which at someone else's wedding could be seen as selfish, but I had reached my threshold of what I could cope with.

I plonked myself into Louise's tiny two-seater and sighed a huge sigh of relief.

'And then the kids started throwing balls at each other and one of them got hit in the face!' Louise said as she banged on about something that had happened at her work. I looked over to her and felt calm and warm (probably from the heated car seats, seriously, Louise, my arse is always on fire in your car), and in that moment everything that I had been through in the last week, in the last eight hours, in the last year, wasn't an issue anymore.

After a very emotionally charged day I finally felt calm and safe being driven back to the new life that I'm still carving out for myself. A life that sometimes feels uncomfortable and uncertain, but one that is full of hope, love and happiness. So as Louise banged on further about whatever it was she was banging on about, I smiled to myself.

Oh sure, when I got home I crumbled and fell to pieces (well, I had consumed a hell of a lot of alcohol) and I cried my eyes out over everything that I had lost this year. Yes, I've lost over three stone, but I've also lost my Cat, my fluffy children and everything that seemed familiar and normal.

For the sake of my mental and physical health, I think I'll give alcohol a miss for the foreseeable future. It doesn't serve me anymore and I only need things that serve me in life – like servants and sexy black waistcoats.

My friend's wedding was the perfect ending to what had been an overwhelming year and I think that's why I bawled my eyes out. It's taken everything I had and everything I didn't have (or *know* that I had) to sort my life out and get through this year.

SCREWED UP, SLIMMED DOWN

Your new life is going to cost you your old one.
It's going to cost you your comfort zone and your sense
of direction.
It's going to cost you relationships and friends.
It's going to cost you being liked and understood.
It doesn't matter.
The people who are meant for you are going to meet you
on the other side. You're going to build a new comfort
zone around the things that actually move you forward.
Instead of being liked, you're going to be loved. Instead of
being understood, you're going to be seen.
All you're going to lose is what was built for a person you
no longer are

Brianna Wiest

CHAPTER 49

WREATH IT AND WEEP

It's Christmas Day! Sing it with me: *Chriiiiiistmas tiiiiiime, mistletoe and whine*-ing, *lots* of whining… But not from me; no, no, from my dad. This year I invited *both* of my divorced parents to spend Christmas in my little flat and my dad has, let's say, 'strong views' on how I should be cooking the roast potatoes.

Dad's method of cooking roast potatoes:

Step 1: Place your special roast potato tin into the oven and heat it to 200 degrees Celsius.

Step 2: Delicately peel 1kg of potatoes and cut each potato into four pieces.

Step 3: Lovingly drop the potatoes into a large pan and slowly pour in enough water to cover them.

Step 4: Add some Himalayan pink salt to the water and bring it to a boil. Once the potatoes are dancing in the pan, lower the heat and keep it at a simmer.

SCREWED UP, SLIMMED DOWN

Step 5: Put 100 grams of organic goose fat into your special roast potato tin and heat it in the oven.

Step 6: Drain the potatoes by using a colander, then tenderly shake the colander to allow the potatoes to fluff up like pretty little clouds.

Step 7: Sprinkle two tablespoons of flour onto the potatoes from a great height. Then give them another quick shimmy-shake so that they are evenly covered.

Step 8: Kindly place the potatoes into the hot fat and then roll them around so that every single aspect of the potato is coated. Ensure to give each potato plenty of room to cook.

Step 9: Roast the heavenly carb in the oven for 3 x 15 minute intervals, taking them out to turn them over meticulously in between each interval.

Step 10: Once the delicious starchy diamonds are golden and crisp, take them out of the oven, scatter them with fresh and zesty lemon flavoured Cornish sea salt and then serve them straightaway.

My method of cooking roast potatoes:

Step 1: Open bag of frozen roast potatoes.

Step 2: Put in oven.

Step 3: Serve 30 minutes later.

My dad only lives an hour's drive away from my place; however, he doesn't like driving in the dark, in the rain or in reverse, so he has given me a very specific timeframe in which he will be at mine for Christmas: between the hours of 10 am and 2 pm. After which he will be driving home before the sun sets and then spending the rest of the festive day plonked in front of the TV watching the 24-hour news channel. What is it with dads and watching the news all the time? At what age does that become a thing? As soon as a dad hits 60, BAM, the news channel is on and it never goes off.

My mum, on the other hand, lives down in Dorset, and while she *also* doesn't drive in the dark, in the rain or in reverse, she doesn't actually drive at all. So she's staying with me for a few days, which is of course lovely and not at all a challenge. Yes, I've lived on my own for six months now, but that doesn't mean that I'm *so* set in my ways that anyone coming into my home and changing the position of my toilet roll is going to turn me into a fiery, raging bitch. No, no. I am Zen.

'How long until lunch?' Dad yelled from his spot on the sofa for the third time.

'Father dearest, you keeping asking is not going to make it appear any quicker. You'll know when lunch is ready when it's in front of you,' I replied from the kitchen as I carefully squished the parsnips onto the oven tray that was already overloaded with the salmon wellington and a million roast potatoes. When you live on your own you only need *one* oven dish, and to be fair I hadn't really thought this bit through when I offered to cook a big fat roast for three people. So what if the parsnips, potatoes and wellington all squish together as one? It's going to end up that way in their stomachs anyway…

I haven't spent Christmas Day with both of my parents since I was a one-year-old and to be honest my memory of that time is somewhat hazy. I imagine I just cried, ate and slept all day. What a dream…

Growing up, I always spent Christmas Day with my mum and Boxing Day with my dad, but when I became an adult I tried my best to alternate who I saw on Christmas Day. However, when Cat and I were together we then had

SCREWED UP, SLIMMED DOWN

to alternate some more. Luckily her parents were still together so we didn't have to do four lots of alternating, just three. And now it's back to just me I can kill two birds with one giant frozen roast potato and see them both at the same time.

I knew that the day might be a little challenging, what with it being the first Christmas without Cat, so I got up early and went for a run along the beach, which helped get rid of any anxious energy that I had and also made me feel smug as fuck. That's right, I'm so into health and fitness that I go running on Christmas Day. I'm basically Kelly Holmes. (Good topical reference there, Jenna – Kelly Holmes, an Olympic athlete who retired in 2005.)

Throughout the day I'd also planned other activities, like a bike ride, in order to keep me busy enough so that my mind didn't have time to sit and reminisce. Also, I had my parents to worry about, and that was going to help occupy my mind as well.

Thankfully, my divorced parents do get on well enough to spend a few unsupervised hours together while their second-born, aka me, the favourite, makes them a delicious Christmas roast dinner.

'I'm buying and I'm cooking, so I'll hear zero complaints,' I announced when I sent the invite.

Christmas is a bit of a bastard though, isn't it? There's so much expectation to be happy, be social, be fun, be drunk, be fed, be generous, be this, be that! Blah blah blah... But what if I just want to eat junk food on the sofa on my own and not communicate with anyone other than the earwigs in my flat? When does Jenna get to live *her* dream Christmas?

My dream Christmas, for those who are eager for me to elaborate, would start with me having Baileys on my cereal – it's Jesus's birthday and intermittent fasting doth not apply on Jesus's birthday. I'd then spend the morning going between picking the blackheads on my face, dancing around my living room to Spanish Christmas songs and watching tennis montage videos on the TV. By 3 pm I'd have eaten my festive lunch, which would be a banging homemade halloumi burger with chips and baked beans, and then by 7 pm I'd be an immovable object drunk on chocolate.

Once I'd regained the ability to move my limbs, I'd then plop myself into the bath where I'd enjoy a packet of biscuits and old episodes of *Will & Grace* on my iPad. I'd then spend the rest of the evening splashing about while reciting every word of *Will & Grace*, making myself laugh so much that I'd spill loads of biscuit crumbs in the bath.

But we do not live in Jenna's dream world just yet, so Christmas this year was spent with both parents sitting on the sofa waiting to be fed while I was in the kitchen cooking dinner and shouting out conversation starters so that my parents didn't sway onto anything too controversial – such as politics, Covid or my decision to quit my job and live off my savings, which are quickly running out.

'What do you think about your firstborn's decision to grow an Amish beard?' I yelled from the kitchen, trying to cut the carrots as quietly as possible so that I could still monitor their conversation.

'Dinner is ready!' I finally announced, coming out of the kitchen with their plates full to the brim with carbs and a small serving of carrots plonked on top. 'There's no cranberry sauce and that's all the gravy I've got, so if you want something to keep the food moist then may I suggest that one of you makes yourself useful and gets the mayonnaise out of the fridge,' I said, placing the plates in front of my parents who both wore their best fake smiles.

Surprisingly my first homemade Christmas dinner got rave reviews and during the meal there were *zero* complaints – no one even mentioned the fact that the parsnips were burnt because I'd put them so close to the edge of the oven dish that they were basically flame-grilled.

'Thanks for lunch, Bubba,' my dad said as he hugged

me goodbye. 'Next time stop being so cheap and buy another oven dish so your mother and I don't have to eat cremated parsnips.' Dammit, I thought I'd gotten away with it. 'I love you, I'll text you when I get home.'

'Did your dad have a nice time?' my mum asked me when I returned to the lounge.

'Yeah, I think so. Did you two have a nice time chatting while I was slaving away in the kitchen?'

'Yeah, we were just talking about old times, the people we used to know and about how well you've done this year.'

'Aw, that's nice, thank you.'

My relationship with my family has definitely gotten better this year, mainly because I've added boundaries (like me not staying at my brother's house) and I've learnt to be more patient and not let myself get so wound up or upset by their words (like when my mum asks how I'll feel when Cat starts dating again).

'I'm proud of what you done this year,' my mum said, rubbing my arm. Was she talking about my weight loss, my breakup or my mental health transformation? Who cares, it's a compliment, take it!

'Thanks, Mum,' I said, smiling.

'Well, I know it's not been easy and you've managed to lose all that weight.' Ah, she was talking about my weight loss. 'I'm still trying to lose a few pounds…' she said as she pushed the remaining Quality Street chocolates around in the box.

'It's definitely been a challenge to lose weight, especially going through all the mental health stuff as well, but I feel really good and I can finally fit into all of those goal clothes that I've bought over the years.'

'Oh, that's good. You definitely don't need to lose any more,' she told me, unwrapping the last purple Quality Street.

I texted Cat wishing her and her family a Merry Christmas and a few hours later she replied wishing me the

SCREWED UP, SLIMMED DOWN

same. I thought I'd be sadder on the first Christmas without her, but I'm moving on and I, thankfully, was so busy worrying about how my parents would be with each other that I didn't have time to dwell on the fact that she wasn't here.

I got through Christmas Day without a single tear, without a single argument and without a single drop of alcohol. Woo hoo! It's fair to say that my early morning run along the beach really set me up well for the day, and then the bike ride that I had after lunch really set me up well for the rest of the afternoon. And then the two-hour bath that I had after the bike ride really set me up well for the evening. Exercise is the best distraction.

Christmas is tough, but it's important to remember that not everyone is surrounded by family at Christmas. The lucky bastards…

CHAPTER 50

THANK FUCK THAT'S OVER

January

Well sod me sideways, I've only gone and made it through the entire transformational year. Well done me, can we all have a big clap! Alright, that's enough, calm down… It's currently 12:15 am on New Year's Day and I'm feeling as smug as a pig with two dicks. I don't know if that's the saying, but that's how smug I'm feeling.

I've taken back control of my life, control of my physical and mental health and it's been a huge bollocking struggle, but I've done it. I'm now 12 and a half stone, my belly is under 37 inches in circumference and I've been panic-attack free for four wonderful months. To celebrate my most excellent achievement, I'm going to buy myself a Rafael Nadal tennis jacket, not because it will finally look good on me now that I'm thinner, but because I have finally realised that me and my inner child are worthy of nice things. And if I want to spend £70 on a thin piece of branded material that will probably break in a month then I *will* spend £70 on a thin piece of branded material that will probably break in a month. Self-love, innit.

Throughout this year I've gone on a journey from being a people-pleasing quiet little goose with minimal friends, to someone who is still slightly people-pleasing and quite goose-like but who is now much more her authentic self. I, without boasting, now need *all* of my fingers to count the number of friends I have. OK, you could cut off maybe one or two, but please don't because I need them to write my much anticipated second book after this one becomes an instant bestseller. Manifestation, bbz, let's try it.

Being panic-attack free feels incredible. I've come to realise that there are certain things in life that trigger my panic attacks: mainly experiencing feelings of being stuck, living a life that isn't true to me, being in a place where I feel out of control and also, staying at other people's houses. I don't know why I don't like staying at other people's houses but there's something about not having the ability to leave whenever I want to that makes me feel like a trapped little bunny.

Amazingly, I made it through the Christmas and New Year period without putting my head in the oven with the fake turkey, *nor* did I use alcohol to numb my feelings and I *only* had *half* a ton of chocolate. Yes, I am an inspiration.

Thanks to my new sobriety, I went for a run at midnight on New Year's Eve instead of getting absolutely plastered. There's no feeling quite like running along the beach at night watching all the fireworks in Brighton explode in the distance. God, it's orgasmic.

As I was running along the beach in the horrendous wind and rain (Wanda convinced me to go out for a run even though the weather was biblical and I'm glad I listened to her), the fireworks over Brighton Pier exploded into a beautiful array of colour and noise and I stopped running for a bit to take in the scene with my arms outstretched like I was Kate in *Titanic*.

Hazel Dean's 'They Say It's Going to Rain' was playing in my headphones, the rain was smacking me in the face and I had a huge smile – I've fucking done it. I've put myself first, I did the two hardest things that I could ever do (those two things being losing weight and going through a breakup that nearly broke me, for those who *seriously* haven't been paying attention). The elation, joy and relief that raced through my body was euphoric.

'Happy New Year!' a gaggle of teenagers yelled at me as I ran past them while they were taking a selfie and doing the underage drinking.

'Happy New Year, woo hoo!' I yelled back, full of all the happy chemicals. I ran further down the beach back towards my flat.

'Happy New Year!' a gaggle of old people yelled at me as I ran past them while they were taking a selfie and doing the age-appropriate drinking.

'Happy New Year! Woo hoo!' I yelled back. God, isn't everyone so bloody friendly? Are they always this friendly? Do teenagers normally say hello? Well, then, maybe I shall try interacting with them more often!

When I started this journey 12 months ago, I thought it was just going to be about losing weight and that was going to be a big bastard challenge in itself, but no, life and the Universe had other plans.

I never thought I'd escape my large fleshy prison, I never thought I'd get to a place where I feel hope about the future – and I never thought I'd get to a place where I feel confident enough to ask someone in Lidl if I can go in front of them in the queue because I only have three items. But I *have* and I *do*.

I didn't know before this transformation journey that I wore a mask. But I did, a different mask for the different Jennas depending on who she was with. A mask with different friends, family, colleagues and with Cat. How does this person want me to be? Which Jenna would be acceptable for this person? What is expected of me and how can I meet this expectation?

It didn't matter who *I* wanted to be, or who *I* was inside, I just simply put the masks on, and this year has been about taking them off. And it's uncomfortable, it's hard, it's bloody scary at times, but oh my God, it's the best thing I've ever done.

Later on today (once I've slept off this euphoric buzz from all the wet running), I'm going around to Steve's house for a civilised New Year's Day buffet. All the tennis gang are going to be there and I am just completely myself with these people.

I will talk bollocks, I will make bad jokes and I won't wear a single bloody mask. It'll be awesome and terrifying and I'm not going to lie, after spending time with people without any mask on I may have to spend an hour or two going through all the absolute twatting waffle that came out of my mouth, but that's OK.

> **Wanda:** It's great that you've finally realised that if people don't like your absolute twatting waffle, then they're not your people. The real Jenna deserves real friends.
>
> **Me:** Exactly!
>
> **Earl:** I don't like your absolute twatting waffle, I find it boring and annoying.
>
> **Me:** That's OK, I find you boring and annoying.
>
> **Earl:** Life is boring and—
>
> **Me:** Actually, Earl, I don't need to hear your negativity anymore.
>
> **Earl:** Oh… Why not?
>
> **Me:** Because focusing on death and sadness makes it harder to live and enjoy life, and that's actually what I'm trying to do now.
>
> **Earl:** What's the point of enjoying life if you're going to die?
>
> **Me:** What's the point of eating a banging chocolate fudge cake if it's just going to come out as poo?
>
> **Earl:** Well, it tastes nice on the way in.
>
> **Me:** There you go then, Earl, life ends one day, but that doesn't mean it's not worth enjoying right now.
>
> **Earl:** Oh God, you're right…

At the beginning of the year I was in a long-term relationship, I had a job and I wanted to move to Edinburgh. I'm now single, unemployed and still living in England, but I'm doing good.

I don't know what the future holds (though I hope it's a lot of money, sex and puppies), but next year's goals have got a lot to live up to! I have more weight to lose (about a stone and a half after all that Christmas stuffing – not a euphemism), I need to keep trying to make it as a writer and I want to come off my antidepressants – which is going to be another big bastard challenge: Jenna, conqueror of big bastard challenges.

I will continue to put myself out of my comfort zone, try new things as much as possible and continue on this amazing journey that I've started. It's taken me 33 years, but I'm finally no longer waiting for my real life to begin.

Oh, and next year I might even attempt to join the dating scene again. Holy shit…

CHAPTER 51

THREE DESSERTS AND A BEARD

February
9 am
It's date day. She's a five foot eight PE teacher, she likes country music and we met on Tinder. I wouldn't say that I had high hopes, but I hope that we can agree on wedding venues and going to Nashville for our honeymoon when it comes to that. I'm joking, obviously…

God, I've got to hurry up and get ready for this date. It's just coffee (well, tea because coffee is disgusting) and cake – I must eat cake properly like a civilised human being and not like a greedy ogre who hasn't eaten for a month.

What the hell do you wear for a coffee date? I've just spent 45 minutes trying on everything in my wardrobe that's casual but not 'slob' and smart but not 'wedding'. Must remember to pluck my beard before leaving, it's got a good three days' growth to it and it might give off the impression that I'm a hairy Mary. Which I am, but she doesn't need to know that on the *first* date.

2:30 pm
I don't want to get too ahead of myself, but I think that

blue would be a nice colour theme for our wedding. No, Jenna! Bad Jenna! The date went well, she was charming and relaxed, though I could tell she was a little bit nervous because she kept bouncing her leg up and down.

'What would you like to drink?' she asked. Oh great, she's buying! I wonder how many free drinks I can get out of my dates. Not that it's a game or that I'm planning on creating a fun spreadsheet to see how many freebies I can get, but still…

'A mint tea, please.'

'And what would you like to eat?'

'Oh, umm…' Ever the indecisive goon that I am, I said I was torn between the brownie and the chocolate cake. 'Can I have the brownie, please? Oh, but there's a cookie as well! Actually, yeah, the brownie, please.'

As she ordered the drinks at the counter I got to have a good look at her arse – firm, tight, very nice. Being a PE teacher definitely suits her physique. I also learnt later that she's a triathlete. Oh shit, I'm going to have to up my exercise.

When she came back to the table she had a large plate with one brownie, one chocolate cake and a small cookie on it.

'I know you couldn't decide, so I thought we'd get all of them and share,' she said. Oh, huge bloody brownie points (quite literally, really).

I noticed as she spoke about her love of animals over humans (another tick) that she had a small cross tattooed on her arm. Hmm. I assumed it could be one of two things: one, it's just a cool hip tattoo or two, she's religious and loves the Jesus. It turned out that it was number two, she loves the Jesus.

'It's normally a bit of a tricky point for people,' she said. Not for me though, I'm very open to everyone and everything, apart from Sikhs, the bastards. That's a joke, obviously. It doesn't bother me one little bit if someone is religious, unless they start using it as an excuse to be a sexist homophobe, but as she's a gay woman, the chances of that are, like her legs, quite slim.

'So, what's the guitar tattoo on your arm about, do you play?' she asked, pointing to my big-ass arm tattoo.

'Oh Christ, no.' Jenna, don't say Christ in front of someone who loves the Jesus. 'It's for my love of country music; the guitar strap says Brandi Carlile and The Dixie Chicks. They're my favourite artists,' I said beaming.

'Oh yeah, I remember you said you like country music, that's why I wore my flannel shirt today.'

Oh, hello, not only did she buy me all the cakes but she also dressed in a way that she thought I might find attractive. I mean, she's right, the flannel shirt looked great on her – not as great as those tight jeans, but still, very nice.

'So, what made you get into stand-up comedy?' she asked, taking the smaller half of the brownie (more brownie points, get in!).

'I love to make people laugh.'

'Ah, so you're a manic depressive?' Sorry, how the hell did she get that within 15 minutes of meeting me? Wow… I just laughed into my mint tea, avoiding all eye contact. She doesn't need to know about my funky mental health just yet. Baby steps, darling.

'OK, this might be weird, but I like to guess what month people were born,' I said, changing the conversation completely. Oh yeah, I was totally myself throughout the entire date, saying whatever weird shit came into my head. 'I'm going to guess May.'

She opened her mouth in amazement.

'How did you know that?'

'Well, you've got a sunny disposition, so I thought summer, and May was coming up.'

'OK, but which date was I born?'

'Hmm.' I thought for a moment. The only date in May that means something to me is the 3rd of May because that's the date that Hannah, the woman I was in love with at school, told me to never contact her again. 'The 3rd of May?' I guessed.

'Wow, no, but that was my due date. I was a week late,' she said, thoroughly impressed with this crazy intuition that I've got about people's due dates. I wonder how I can use this skill for evil? I mean… good.

There was a point during the date when our knees touched under the table and neither of us moved our legs away. I looked at her lips and thought, 'Yeah, I could kiss them. I think I'd like to kiss them.' A really good sign! Especially from someone who thought that her vagina had died.

I'd only got parking for three hours, but we chatted for over two so I had to cut her off at one point, telling her that I only had 20 minutes left on my car which was parked a 25-minute walk away.

We hugged and left, and I sprinted back to my car with a huge smile on my face. She was nice, I'd like to see her again. I can imagine going out for dinner with her, going on holiday, taking her to meet my friends.

I'm joking, of course, I'm not going to let myself get carried away or start projecting my dream fantasy lesbian relationship onto her, but as first dates go, it was a winner.

When I got home from the date I got out my little vanity mirror to start picking the blackheads on my face when suddenly I remembered: I'd forgotten to pluck my beard… Shit, I hope she didn't notice.

I don't know if I'll see her again. A second date would be nice but I'm not really ready for another full-on relationship, so I'm not too fussed. I'm still working on myself. Jesus, does the work *ever* end? Also, I'm enjoying having my freedom, being my authentic self and getting out of my comfort zone exploring new things, so a relationship isn't on the top of my priority list. Sure, a kiss or sexy times with a pretty lady with a nice bum would be bloody lovely, but it's not essential for my happiness right now. I can take care of those needs for myself, ya know?

SCREWED UP, SLIMMED DOWN

Jesus, Jenna, too much information… I do apologise.

SCREWED UP, SLIMMED DOWN

ACKNOWLEDGEMENTS

I'd like to begin by thanking Cat. My darling, thank you so much for allowing me to tell my side of what happened. At the beginning of the book I said that I was waiting for my real life to begin, but I see now that my real life had already started, it started when I met you and although things didn't work out, I will always love you.

Thank you to my wonderful friends for your incredible love and support over the last few years, especially those who helped me get this book to where it is, your support has meant the world to me.

A huge thank you to you, dear reader, for reading this book, it's incredibly personal and I hope that you've laughed/cried/taken something meaningful from it.

And lastly, FKA Bitch Face, I'm sorry I called you FKA Bitch Face, I was in a bad place, I'm sure you're great.

SCREWED UP, SLIMMED DOWN

SCREWED UP, SLIMMED DOWN

ABOUT THE AUTHOR

Jenna Wimshurst is a writer of humorous sketches, essays and books about life, mental health and lesbian culture.

View more of her work at www.jennawimshurst.com

Other books by Jenna
The Weight Is Finally Over
How to Be a Lesbian
The Suicides

244

Printed in Great Britain
by Amazon